INTRODUCTION

ADHD: gift or curse? How can so many experts have such profoundly conflicting ideas? Everyone presents compelling studies and facts supporting their respective arguments, yet they can't seem to come together. Dr. Russell A. Barkley, PhD, a well-respected ADHD expert, aggressively argues that ADHD is a deficit. He states that ADHD is most assuredly a disorder, of which there is no cure, and refers to it as "brain damage, often caused by impact to the frontal lobe." Conversely, Dr. Lynn Weiss, PhD, author of *ADD and Creativity*, passionately makes the case that those with ADHD are not disordered, but are, in fact, "gifted." Countless other experts can be found on both sides of this argument. Those making the case that ADHD is a disorder, or "curse," point out the fact that nearly 50% of those in prison have ADHD, as well as nearly 80% of addicts in treatment facilities. On the other hand, the advocates for the "gifts" of ADHD will point to the countless millionaires, billionaires, inventors, and world leaders with ADHD.

I've found the level of passion on both sides of the argument disturbing, to say the least. It borders on hatred for those who oppose their respective viewpoints. I, for one, believe in the adage that says there are <u>three</u> sides to every story: the one side, the opposing side, and the truth. Only by exploring both extremes with an open mind can one ever expect to find truth.

Certainly, there are significant and real challenges that are faced by those dealing with ADHD. However, there appear to be many gifts and unique talents that come from having a mind that thinks differently. So what is the truth, really? One thing is for sure: truth would be impossible to find without going right to the source—so we did. More specifically, this book is the result of the interviews and studies of one hundred people, split equally between addicts and millionaires, over a period of three years. What did we find? In a nutshell, we found that those with ADHD appear to be three times more likely to end up with addictive behaviors than those without it. What was more interesting (and certainly more hopeful) was the discovery that those with ADHD appear to be nearly three times more likely to become extremely successful. Thus the title to the book, *ADDicts and Millionaires*: *The Gifts and Curse of ADHD*. (Note: Though our database of interviewees has grown since the original group, the numbers have remained statistically the same.)

It is my firm belief that the ability to choose between the two paths, ADDict or Millionaire, is always there, IF, and only IF, there is a full understanding of both the gift and the curse of ADHD. To that end we are attempting to educate, so that readers who are affected by ADHD may have a choice.

HEAD'S UP: This introduction is as formal as my writing gets, so don't expect much more of that formality in this book. I'm a bit childish at heart, and I must warn you, I write from my heart.

Mark Patey

Copyright © 2013 by Genius Amplified LLC, Mark Patey, David Nielsen
All rights reserved.
Illustrations Copyright © 2013 by Genius Amplified LLC. All rights reserved.
Equal-Opposite & Genius Amplified TM by Genius Amplified LLC

ACKNOWLEDGEMENTS

I can't possibly thank everyone enough for their help, time, and commitment to this project. However, an attempt I will make. (That sounded like Yoda!)

To all the millionaires and addicts: Thanks for allowing me into your offices (and/or personal prisons) for interviews, and thank you for your time, honesty, and candor. You shared with me wisdom beyond my years, which was truly priceless! Now, let us hope I got some of that into this book! ;) Many of you requested anonymity and that request was, and will always be, respected.

To my wife, Suzy: Special thanks for your love and commitment of more than twenty years, and especially for your support in light of my continual pursuit of nearly every distraction. You're a Godsend, sweetheart. And in case I'm ever chasing a distraction in the future and forget, Happy Anniversary, Happy Birthday, and Merry Christmas. This totally counts, right? At least for one of them, maybe?

To my staff: Thanks for your continual efforts and sometimes futile attempts to keep me focused on this project. It has payed off. We've done something special here, and I couldn't have done it without you. Extra kudos to Matt Gunderson and Joe Carpenter, two ADHDers who stayed focused through to the end.

To Dave Nielsen: You have been the best Equal-Opposite an ADDer like me could ever ask for. (Equal-Opposite is defined later in the book.) We've built some amazing companies together over the last twenty-plus years, and I wouldn't have wanted to do it with anyone else. Well, maybe someone that wasn't taller and better-looking than I am, but still, in life you only get a few favorites, and you're one of my favorites.

To Mikey-Mike, my twin brother from the same mother: I still argue that your being born first doesn't make you wiser, just older! Thanks for tending to the companies when I ditched town to do interviews for, and to work on, this book for days at a time. And in full disclosure, I confess that a lot of the time away from work I was playing. Since you are as ADHD as I am, I know that if you ever get around to reading this book, you will certainly skip this acknowledgements page so I have nothing to worry about. Oh, and I'm the one that put that big scratch in the jet's wingtip. Sorry! :)

To my four wonderful sons: Thanks for being the guinea pigs for my ADHD brain experiments. We will never know how "normal" you might have been. Love you boys!

DISCLOSURE AND DISCLAIMER

I have ADHD, and thus, I have a bias—this I openly admit. However, a word of caution: It would be foolish for anyone to assume that my theoretical conclusions are inaccurate simply because of that bias. It would be equally ridiculous to seek fault in my opinions merely because I disagree with your own opinion on the matter. If you don't like my work because you don't like my hair style or choice of attire, then that's totally understandable since that would be a completely valid reason to negate my studies. (That's sarcasm, folks.) Science is full of opinions that evolve and shift. My hope is only that this may be one of those discussions worthy of a significant shift. Toward that end I work, while remaining open to being wrong and searching only for truth. After all, taking insult from a theory is an example of precisely what stifles science as a field. Furthermore, ignoring a model because it violates the status quo or is politically insensitive is just bad science. I recognize that much of what I put forward in this book will offend the experts, yet I feel no guilt. Some experts are blind to not see the gifts of the ADHD mind, so I poke experts in the eye daily, blinding them in the hope that they can learn to see differently. Do I feel badly for the proverbial poke in the eye? No. What I feel is only righteous indignation. After a lifetime of being told that I'm broken, that I'm disabled, or that I have a disorder, it feels good to come back with a lifetime of evidence that tells me that I'm not, and neither are the millions of other gifted youth and adults who are blessed with the gift of a brain that does things differently. The ADHD gift.

I am not a doctor, a therapist, or a psychologist, and I am neither licensed nor certified to make any recommendations as to therapy methods, medication, or the like. I state my opinions as such—only opinions. Please take my thoughts and analysis of the things I've learned from studying ADHD addicts and millionaires at face value. I'm completely honest in my assessments of my data, but I recognize that honesty doesn't truth make. Question everything and everyone, evaluate all opinions for yourself and your circumstances, and make up your own mind.

Most importantly, I personally think that rabbits are less threatening than turtles—and much softer, too.

CHAPTER 1

SOULS ON BOARD

*"Center, this is niner-eight-five-three golf.
We may be in a bit of trouble here."*

I recall a particularly memorable flight one cold and rainy winter evening. I had been asked to speak at a conference in Southern California, and I was in a hurry to get to Utah for another speaking engagement I had the next morning in Salt Lake City. My twin brother, Mike, and I examined the weather conditions and aviation forecasts and, after careful consideration, decided we would make the trip,

DISTRACTION: In aviation, direction is described in terms of compass points. 030 would reference northeast.

knowing that there could be possible icing during part of our climb to altitude. We would fly Mike's plane, a large twin-engine aircraft equipped for all types of weather, including flight into known icing conditions. We took off and the ride was bumpy—much worse than had been forecasted. On our way through 18,000 feet we hit turbulence so violent that my flight bag hit the ceiling on multiple occasions. About that time, the

Ice on a plane wing = bad

autopilot alarm sounded as a result of its inability to maintain control of the aircraft. Mike disengaged the autopilot and flew the plane manually until smoother air could be found. Mike joked, "I'm glad we don't have any friends with us; they would be freaking out right now." We laughed for a bit as we reminisced about another flight that resulted in a good friend losing bodily fluids out both ends during a business/pleasure trip. We continued our climb through an altitude of 25,000 feet, which put us safely above the icy weather below. On top of the clouds, the air was calm and smooth, the sky was clear, and the moon and stars were as bright as ever. The contrast from only seconds earlier was stark. Everyone always says it's calmest before the storm, but I find the opposite to be more true: it's after the greatest turbulence in life that the calm is really noticed and appreciated.

DISTRACTION:
A TRANSPONDER IN AN AIRCRAFT IS A GADGET THAT GIVES OFF AN IDENTIFYING SIGNAL

Mike reengaged the autopilot, and turned on the XM radio for entertainment during the remaining hour of our trip home.

As we normally do, we had the secondary

communications radio in the aircraft tuned to the emergency frequency, 121.5. Many pilots will do this just in case someone is in need of help. If it ever came to that we could try to assist, or we could listen for any ELTs (emergency locator transmitters) and report them to the air traffic controllers. After thousands of flight hours and never hearing anyone call for emergency assistance, we were both shocked as the following words came clearly over the radio:

"**Center, this is niner-eight-five-three golf. We may be in a bit of trouble here.**"

Center then returned, "**Five-three golf, are you declaring an emergency?**"

Once a pilot declares an emergency, he or she is given priority handling and is allowed to deviate from any flight rules or procedures in order to help him or her safely complete the flight.

"**Ah, yeah, I think this is an emergency. We are flying blind and picking up ice. I'm no longer able to maintain normal air speed.**"

No pilot ever wants to admit they need help. I think it's human nature to want to do things on our own, but in this case the failure to call for help certainly leads to only one outcome . . . and it's fatal.

"**. . . Five-three golf, set transponder *squawk* 7700 and do your best to maintain airspeed.**"

Turning your transponder to 7700 helps ATC (air traffic control) know which one of all the blips on their radar display is the plane in an emergency, and enables them to track and better assist the troubled flight.

The pilot replied, "***squawk* 7700, but I can't maintain airspeed. I would like to descend into some warmer air**

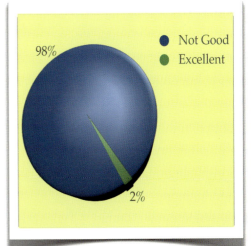

Chart 1.1 *Chances of Surviving Life While Making Bad Choices*

below. Can I descend?"

Air temperatures change about 3.8 degrees Fahrenheit for every thousand feet in altitude change. If a pilot descends 5000 feet the temperature will rise roughly 19 degrees, giving them much better odds of melting the ice off the wings and airframe. The controller came back with a haunting reply.

"Negative five-three golf, I've got radar contact showing you over the Rocky Mountains. If I clear you for any lower, I can't guarantee you terrain clearance."

> "SEVERAL MINUTES WENT BY AND NOTHING WAS HEARD FROM THE PILOT. THE REALIZATION THAT I HAD JUST WITNESSED THE DEATH OF FOUR SOULS WAS TAKING ROOT ... "

Mike and I looked at each other in disbelief. "These guys are already dead," I commented while shaking my head. Mike finished my thoughts the way only a twin brother could with, ". . . and they just don't know it yet."

My mind was filled with memories of flights I had taken that were in questionable weather conditions, as well as flights I had cancelled for the same reasons. I would rather be on the ground wishing I was flying than in the air wishing I was on the ground. As with many things in life, one wrong choice at the wrong time and it's all over. The reality was that these people were dead the second the pilot chose to fly that night. The rest of the journey was just more of the same bad choices, with the biggest one being the choice to not turn around the very instant it looked bad. Life is exactly the same. Course correction must be a constant.

The pilot came back quickly with a strong voice. **"Center, I've got to descend to maintain airspeed! We're losing it here!"**

The controller replied, **"Maintain your current heading for another minute or so and I can give you a slight turn to the right with a descent."**

"Roger, waiting for the right turn and descent."

Although it was only moments, it seemed like an hour before the controller came back on the radio. It must have felt like a lifetime for the pilot and his passengers.

"Niner-eight-five-three golf, be ready for a right turn to heading zero-three-zero on my mark."

The pilot replied with obvious panic in his voice. "**Roger. Heading 030 on your mark. We're ready.**"

"Now, five-three golf! Turn immediately to the right, heading 030!"

The pilot replied, "**Turning now, 030, and I'm already descending. I can't keep my airspeed!**"

"Understood. Do your best to descend only as much as you must to maintain a safe airspeed. I'm sending you through a small canyon and might lose radio contact with you until you're on the other side."

I can't begin to imagine what was going through that pilot's mind when he realized he would be descending through a canyon, at night, with an iced-up plane and no radio contact for course corrections. I had just come through the same weather in a bird that was built for it and it still had my heart rate up. And then came the next question from the controller—the one question that no pilot ever wants to hear as it's often the last question a controller will ask:

Choose your course wisely.

"Five-three golf... how many souls on board?"

There was an eerie silence on the radio before the pilot responded, slowly and quietly.

"Four. Four souls on board."

As painful as it was to listen to, I loved and will always love that question. In a world consumed with political correctness a phrase stemming back to the early days of flight and war, that certainly would make many an atheist uncomfortable, is still appropriately asked when someone is in dire need. *How many souls on board!* Of course, in aviation the question itself is asked because there is usually nothing left when a plane hits the ground. I know, because in my years of search and rescue service I've had to pick up what's left of plane crashes in the unforgiving Utah Rockies. It helps to know how many bodies were on the plane as there is little left to identify.

In our regular, day-to-day lives, I feel this question is even more important, for the resulting outcome of people's lives is so much more than just life and death. It's a question of souls—loved or lost, happy or tormented, devastated by circumstance or hopeful as a result of individual efforts.

"What kind of man would live where there is no daring? I don't believe in taking foolish chances, but nothing can be accomplished without taking any chance at all."
-Charles Lindberg

I can't help but think of my life, my family, my faith, or my businesses, and ask myself the very same question. How many souls on board? How many are looking to me for leadership, for an example, or to help them through a tough time? Am I on the right course? Or more importantly, am I aware enough to recognize if I'm off course? Am I humble enough to ask for help? Do I know how to tune into the right frequency and listen for guidance from others who are smarter than I? Am I taking others, who are completely innocent, down a dangerous path that I've chosen? Can I, and/or will I, choose to survive? And (perhaps most importantly) when possible, am I helping others whom I see on the wrong path to course correct? This book is largely the result of this very question haunting my mind on many sleepless nights.

Several minutes went by and nothing was heard from the pilot. The realization that I had just witnessed the death of four souls was taking root, and I began to wonder if I would be called out on the search efforts upon landing. I was sick. If only they had not gone. Didn't they look at the weather forecasts? Didn't they know the plane they were flying couldn't handle icing conditions? Why didn't they just turn around sooner?

Just then my thoughts were interrupted by what sounded like screaming over the radio.

The controller responded, **"Niner-eight-five-three golf, was that you?"**

Again came screaming over the radio, but we still couldn't understand what was being said. The controller, more firmly now, repeated, **"Niner-eight-five-three golf, IS THAT YOU?!"**

The reply was the last thing any of us expected.

"Yes . . . yes, Center, it's us! We can see the ground! I can see the highway below us . . . I think we are going to make it!"

A short break in the radio traffic gave Mike and I just enough time to make eye contact. I remember his shocked look, the smile in his eyes.

"The ice is coming off . . . we are going to make it! We are going to make it!"

This pilot was screaming for joy; his passengers were celebrating in the background; my brother and I, who didn't even know these people, were celebrating as if we were in the cabin with them. And, I am certain, somewhere, wherever that controller was, he was doing the same. A miracle, truly, but one must wonder what might have happened if they hadn't asked for help. Or, if the controller—the expert—had been slightly off with his directions and had suggested heading 020. That's still almost the same thing as 030, but the result would have been disastrous.

I'm writing this because I believe the directions given to many with ADD/ADHD are just enough off course to be disastrous. They're so close, but sometimes close isn't good enough. There are, however, people out there who have been through the same storm you may find yourself in now, and they have figured a few things out along the way about coping, living, and thriving—and they're standing by, waiting for your call.

May we all find a center to call into. May we all be humble enough to ask for and accept help. May we listen to voices wiser than our own, and may we never forget the words from an inspired controller:

"HOW MANY SOULS ON BOARD?"

Big Questions:
1. What's the outcome of the course I'm currently on?
2. Do I need to course correct?
3. Am I looking to the right sources for guidance?

SOULS ON BOARD Takeaways:
- ✓ Recognize you're not alone.
- ✓ Don't be afraid to ask for help.
- ✓ Often, it's the little corrections that count the most.
- ✓ As you learn to navigate, step up and help others course-correct.
- ✓ Never underestimate your ability to be an influence.

Thank you, Control!

YOUR GENIUS, AMPLIFIED!

(After nearly every chapter, you'll find a wrap-up that goes over the important points made, and hopefully adds some extra insight to help build up your already impressive smarts. Read on, genius!)

The ADHD Three Cs:

1. Consider your source

2. Collaborate

3. Continually course correct

Consider Your Source. Finding success with ADHD is no different than learning to fly and getting a pilot's license. When learning to fly, you first consider your source, or who you are going to trust your life with. You wouldn't take diet advice from someone who has a charge account at McDonald's, right? So would you choose to jump in the plane for your first lessons on take-offs and landings with the college professor who has a PhD in Aviation Science but has never actually flown an airplane, or would you choose an instructor who has substantial flight hours? Taking it further, what if your choice was a new flight instructor with limited experience in the plane you'll be flying, or an instructor that has thousands of hours in that make and model aircraft, and has demonstrated him or herself a master aviator? This should be an obvious decision. If you took the most educated aviation expert in the world, with every possible PhD, and put him at the controls instead of Captain Sully, the result would assuredly have been "Death on the Hudson" instead of "The Miracle on the Hudson." (Not sure what I'm referring to? Google it. Incredible story.) However, ADHDers repeatedly make an equivalent error by taking the bulk of their advice from those who do not have ADHD and can't fully relate, or from those who have ADHD but have found no real, meaningful successes in life.

Collaborate. Once you've considered the source and chosen an instructor, you will find yourself in the cockpit, collaborating with that instructor on nearly every aspect of the flight as you gain experience.

Remember these three Ps (yeah, it's kind of a theme with us): Learn a Principle, Practice it, and Perfect the principle in preparation for your first solo flights.

Continually course correct. Finally, you're flying solo and you've learned that it's impossible to complete any flight without continual course correction. Winds change, weather moves in, and even the aircraft can have troubles. You must continually adjust your course to achieve success. Luckily for the ADHD brain, we are fine with jumping around a bit. One might say our entire lives are a series of course corrections. But that's a good thing.

In aviation, fail to consider your source and you will die. Fail to collaborate while you're learning and you will die once out on your own. Fail to continually course correct and you will die. Emotional, spiritual, financial, social, and even physical death already plague ADHDers. Hasn't there been enough?

> "Life is not a solo act. It's a huge collaboration, and we all need to assemble around us the people who care about us and support us in times of strife"
> -Tim Gunn

CHAPTER 2

THE MISSING LINK

Confession: I'm nervous writing this chapter. I feel inadequate, even unworthy, to properly put into words the depth and breadth of what I need to write next. Even the title of this chapter isn't right, or at least misses the full gravity and importance of what is to follow. I wish I were an educated writer, with a greater grasp of the English language and its proper usage. I wish I had the words to capture what is in my heart and mind.

ADDicts and Millionaires—what sets them apart? What key pieces of the puzzle are missing or different between the ultra-successful and those languishing in self-loathing and/or self-destruction? I've always believed you can tell a lot about someone by the company they keep. Perhaps this is the best place to begin our study of the ADDicts and Millionaires.

My work to interview 100 people for this book started with people I know, or more specifically, my peers. They were the easiest to get time with, and more importantly, to get an open and honest dialog rolling. I consider myself fortunate to know a lot of very successful people, and whenever possible I spend time with them, knowing that the beliefs and value systems that govern their decisions and directions in life will rub off on me in a positive way. We will always become more and more like those we spend the most time with. It's a simple law: if you want to be happier in life, spend time with happy people. Want to be wealthy? Rub shoulders with those who are wealthy. This really is nothing new to most of you reading this book, I only bring it up to better set the stage for the bombshell I'm going to drop here shortly. A discovery, really—THE discovery, or

A good E.O. can help you focus your awesome ideas into something workable.

awareness, of a certain type of person that was present in the life of each and every millionaire interviewed for this book (or **ADDers**, as I'll be calling them. An ADDer is someone leveraging their ADHD gift to their advantage, and is contributing, or "adding," to the world around them.), and absent in the life of each of the **ADDicts** (pretty much the opposite of an ADDer.)

      I had conducted only a dozen or so interviews with millionaires when I first became aware of an unusually consistent theme. What shocked me wasn't that there was a common theme. I had expected that, and toward that end I was researching for this book, specifically in hopes to find commonalities in personality traits, beliefs, and behaviors. What came as such a surprise was that the beliefs, value systems, and behaviors of the millionaires wasn't that common or consistent at all, but rather there was a person in the life of each of the ADHD millionaires that was so consistent I was forced to take notice. And not just take notice, but also document, categorize, and even name the associated personality. It seemed to me as if someone had created the perfect companion to the ADHD individual, and that if you could simply copy and paste that companion into the

Go easy on the finger pointing.

life of almost anyone with ADHD, the end result would be success, happiness, even love. I call these people Equal-Opposites.

Again, the Equal-Opposite (E.O.) was the constant in the ADHD millionaires, or ADDers, interviewed for this book. Sadly, it was also consistently absent in the lives of the ADDicts. That's not to say there wasn't someone who could have been an Equal-Opposite to the ADDict, it's just that any potential E.O.s were unable to see the ADHD individual as an equal. In fact, it was often quite the contrary—they were actively engaged in trying to "fix" the ADHD, and in doing so, inadvertently hurt the very person they were trying to help.

So what is an Equal-Opposite? It's exactly what it sounds like: an equal to the ADDer and yet still completely opposite in how his or her mind functions. They are the organized, detailed, time-sensitive, scheduled, planned structure to the ADDer's creative, spontaneous, turn-on-a-dime, big picture, problem-solving personality. The yin to the yang, as it were, for the ADHD personality.

An Equal-Opposite can be found anywhere. They are often the business partner of an ADDer, but I also saw amazing Equal-

An E.O. often points out things you might not have thought of.

Opposites in the role of secretary. And of course a number of the ADDers' spouses were perfect E.O. partners. In fact, all three roles were found in the lives of many of the ADHD millionaires. Next to every ADDer you will find at least one Equal-Opposite. However, I find it so sad when all too often I see someone who could be or should be an Equal-Opposite not stepping up to the role.

I recently sat down at my favorite steakhouse with a business partner for dinner. When our hostess came for our drink order we recognized each other from times past. The expected small talk was replaced with,

> **DISTRACTION:**
> **ONLY 20 - 30% OF CHILDREN WITH ADHD WILL "OUTGROW" IT. MOST WILL HAVE IT INTO ADULTHOOD.**

"I understand you're researching ADHD for a book you're writing?"

I said yes, and she unloaded . . . It was obvious she was at her wit's end with her husband. She went on and on about how their marriage was about to end as a result of her husband's ADHD. How he kept starting businesses and not following through, would miss important appointments, deadlines . . . on and on. After listening, I took about ten minutes to explain the Equal-Opposite concept to her, and then asked if he had an Equal-Opposite in his business or personal life. She was quiet for a moment, then said something quite profound. Humbly, even sadly, she replied,

"I guess I'm the opposite, but I've never seen him as an equal. I almost have to babysit him. If I didn't tell him to get out of the house he would never be on time to work, and if I didn't remind him of our kids' birthdays he would forget."

I followed up by commenting that the fact that she used the term "babysitting" certainly shows she didn't see him as an equal. I also asked how must that belittlement make him feel, what might it do to his self-worth, confidence, and drive. I then followed up with another question for her.

"Does he possess any talents that you don't?"

Her reply was instant. "Yes. He is super creative, he can find a solution to any problem, he is the constant optimist, an incredible salesman, and he sees things and opportunities others don't."

My follow-up question to her is one I would ask of all you would-be Equal-Opposites:

"Then why is it okay for him to have mental talents and skills you don't possess, but not okay with you if he doesn't possess all the mental talents and skills you have?"

We are all different, and **different is not a disorder** (remember that). Work to magnify your skills, and help your companions magnify their skills. We are not broken, so stop trying to convince us we are. Instead, work with each other's respective talents, as a team, equally! The only thing you will get out of trying to turn your husband into you is a divorce. Opposites attract, and that's a good thing! Trying to fix what makes you opposites will only cause breakage.

Months later, I ran into her again at a mall. She went out of her way to grab me and thank me. She explained that what I had said about Equal-Opposites had haunted her for days, and she decided that instead of worrying and being angry that her husband would forget an appointment, she would just take the role of Equal-Opposite and call him in advance and remind him. At first she said it was hard not to be bugged, because after all,

"Why can't he just remember like the rest of us?"

But then she started to see more and more that his talents were just in different places, and in many ways so much more valuable than just remembering a date. She had embraced her role as an Equal-Opposite, and more importantly, embraced her husband's role as her Equal-Opposite. If you are the one with ADHD, find your Equal-Opposites and you will find success. If you have the mind of an Equal-Opposite, find someone with ADHD. I know there are a lot of ADHD business owners and millionaires who are dying to make you part of their team. Walt Disney (ADHD) had his older brother, Roy—a perfect E.O. Bill Gates (ADHD) had Paul Allen. (Bill's business plan? He admittedly didn't have one, other than to find the smartest people he knew and invite them to partner with him.) Orville Wright (ADHD) had his brother, Wilber. Steve Jobs (ADHD) had Steve Wozniak. Sir Richard Branson (ADHD), founder of the Virgin Group of companies, has had a number of E.O.s, and recently said, "Smart phone? I prefer a brilliant assistant." And author/serial entrepreneur Mark Patey (ADHD) has Suzy Patey (Wife Extraordinaire) and long-time business partner Dave Nielsen (E.O. Par Excellence).

I finish this chapter right where I started. Feeling inadequate, knowing that what I have seen and discovered in the Equal-Opposite ADHD partnership deserves a book of its own. A chapter doesn't begin to scratch the surface of what it means to be an Equal-Opposite as a school teacher, a spouse, a business partner, an employee, or the parent of a child with ADHD. Someday I will give the Equal-Opposite the attention it fully deserves, but for now, I only ask that you open your mind to the possibilities contained in a union between an energetic ADHD brain and a structured Equal-Opposite brain. Together, you can work wonders.

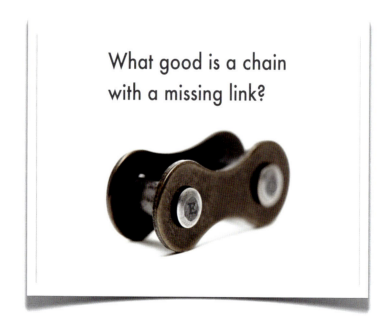

YOUR GENIUS, AMPLIFIED!

The ADHD Three Ls:

1. Link
2. Love
3. Leverage

Link. There is no limit to the levels of success that can be found when you link the ADHD personality with a good Equal-Opposite. The hyper-creative abstract thinker, with the detailed and organized process planner. This link is a formal bond, as in a marriage, a business partnership, or a contract between employer and employee. These links are found everywhere. Of the fifty millionaires interviewed for this book, most of them had ADHD, with E.O.s as either a business partner or high-level managers. Of the millionaires interviewed who were not ADHD, it was interesting to find that they had someone with ADHD within their immediate circle of influence. Make the link.

Love. It's not enough for ADDers and E.O.s to form a professional relationship. They must move to the next level and have a mutual love and respect for each other's differences. Those differences should be celebrated. Sadly though, today's world not only lacks the celebration, but in fact often belittles, and even teases those with ADHD. A valuable asset is squashed under the weight of a societal belief that ADHD is nothing more than a curse. How sad.

Leverage. The last and final part to the ADHD Three Ls is where the rubber meets the road, so to speak. E.O.s have unique talents that ADDers are likely never to possess, and the ADDers possess talents and skill sets that E.O.s are unlikely to gain. These different talents should be divided, and leveraged. A detailed, organized, and structured mind is a gift, and yet creativity, by definition, requires a lack of structure!

E.O. + ADDer = Success with boundless possibilities.

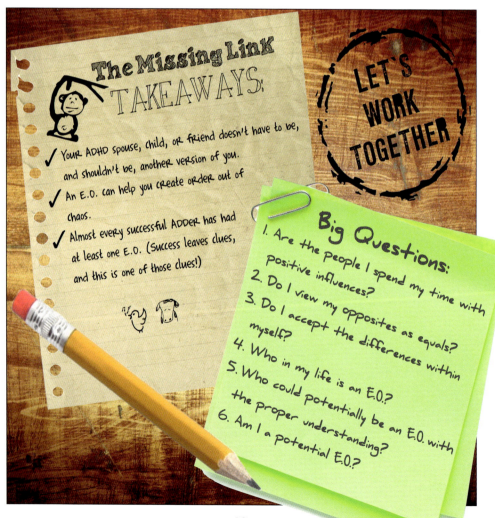

The Missing Link TAKEAWAYS:

- ✓ Your ADHD spouse, child, or friend doesn't have to be, and shouldn't be, another version of you.
- ✓ An E.O. can help you create order out of chaos.
- ✓ Almost every successful ADDer has had at least one E.O. (Success leaves clues, and this is one of those clues!)

LET'S WORK TOGETHER

Big Questions:
1. Are the people I spend my time with positive influences?
2. Do I view my opposites as equals?
3. Do I accept the differences within myself?
4. Who in my life is an E.O.?
5. Who could potentially be an E.O. with the proper understanding?
6. Am I a potential E.O.?

CHAPTER 3

DEADLY BLOWS

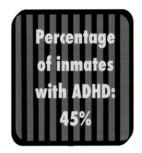

As I have interviewed addicts and millionaires for this book, there has been another constant in every millionaire and an opposite constant in all but two of the addicts. Rarely in any study will you find 100% of anything—there are always too many variables. But surprisingly enough, the results of my survey prove to be an exception.

Every ADHD millionaire I interviewed disagreed with the common understanding that ADHD was entirely a disorder or a deficit, and had on their own decided that the experts were wrong and that the ADHD brain was, in fact, a gift, despite its obvious and glaring challenges. With that said, it's interesting to note that in most cases these men and women didn't like others to know they had ADHD. One mentioned, "It's just too much to overcome in people's perceptions of you." Another commented similarly, "It gets in the way; not the ADHD itself but the way people treat you. There is a lack of confidence that's hard to overcome." I found this fascinating. Keep in mind, these are multi-millionaires. Confident, successful, top-of-the-food-chain kind of people. The average net worth of the ADHD millionaires interviewed for this book was over $20 million, and as far as I can tell it was self-made money. Some of the millionaires interviewed went as far as to say that their ADHD brain was the reason for their success, but still didn't want others to know they have it. However, the few that openly talked about their ADHD with others were the most successful of the group, one of whom's business earned over 50 million dollars a year.

As interesting as that is, I found it even more interesting that the opposite was expressed in the ADHD addicts I talked to. They believed that what their doctors and therapists were telling them was true, that ADHD was simply a mental disorder. Most of the addicts felt that even though they saw benefits in having ADHD, they believed it was, in large part, the cause of their failures. Many of the addicts interviewed went as far as blaming all their life problems on being ADHD. After discovering such a profound difference in the ADHD millionaires and the ADHD addicts, one wonders, why?

Could it be true that by simply disagreeing with the "common knowledge" that ADHD is a disorder, you will increase your chances of success in life? Could the belief that ADHD is a disorder and a deficit be the very cause of your failures in part or whole? I would argue that yes, the above statements are largely true. Discarding the generally accepted notion that ADHD is a disorder is the first of many steps necessary to bring people back from a deadly line of thinking. It's not that simple, though—there's more to it than just following an AA-style program. So let's explore some simple truths about human nature.

The Adventure begins . . .

1982, Northridge Elementary School, my 5th grade classroom: I'm sitting in my chair on the front row, where I was always asked to sit so the teacher could keep a close eye on me. I didn't mind. Ms. Jacobs was my first childhood crush. She was beautiful and nice and so sweet to me. I often imagined that when I grew up she would finally fall in love with me, we would get married, and we'd hold hands all day. Oh, if only I wasn't so much shorter than her, and if only I hadn't wet my pants in the library when the bathrooms were out of order. That couldn't have helped our future romance.

It was reading time and, as usual, I was having a hard time holding still. I had a song in my head I couldn't shake, and as a result I was softly drumming my legs with the palm of my hands under the desk to the beat of the music in my mind. I was still listening to every word as she read from *The Adventures of Huckleberry Finn*, but the song and music played simultaneously in my mind. My crush, Ms. Jacobs, had asked me several times to stop and keep still while she continued to read. I would for a bit, but then, without knowing it, the music was back in my head and I was drumming on my legs again. Finally, she'd had enough. Ms. Jacobs was visibly shaken with frustration. She stood up in the middle of her story, doubled her volume, and exclaimed,

"Mark Patey, we are going to the principal's office! I've had it with you!"

She dropped her book on her desk without even marking the page, and marched my way. *Oh no!* I thought. *What did I do? My future bride is mad at me!* I looked down in horror, finally realizing my possessed hands had been at it again. She grabbed me by one of them and dragged me to the office. I resisted as much as I could, realizing perhaps that this may be the first and only time I'd ever be able to hold hands with her. Oh, the cognitive dissonance! The joy of holding hands, the horror of her being upset at me.

I was dropped off for a chat with the

DISTRACTION:
Of all children who meet the criteria for ADHD, less than half are diagnosed.
- Centers for Disease Control (CDC), 2005

principal, then shortly after, introduced to the school nurse for an interview. She asked a bunch of questions that had nothing to do with my misbehavior in class, so I answered as best I could. It was only a few days later that my parents told me I would be going to another class. I was devastated. I had inadvertently upset my crush so much that she didn't want to ever see me again. Life was over —certainly this is why men commit suicide. My parents tried their best to tell me that my teacher still liked me and that I just needed some special attention only my new teacher could provide, but I still couldn't understand. Who could at that young age?

Days later with books gathered in my arms, the nurse guided me to my new classroom. Maybe it wouldn't be that bad, I told myself. I might make some new friends, and I heard I might get more free time in my new class. However, all hopes of a better experience were replaced with horror when the nurse stopped and grabbed the handle of the special ed. classroom door. *This isn't for me; there's a mistake*, I thought to myself. She must be dropping something off on our way to my new class. But no, the door opened, we entered, and I was introduced. I wanted to cry. My new teacher came over with a huge warm smile on her face, but that didn't help. She crouched down to my level, put one hand on my shoulder, and spoke warmly and very slowly.

My new class? This wasn't it.

"You must be Mark. We are so happy to have you in our class."

I looked at the nurse, confused.

Why was this new teacher talking so slowly to me? What was going on? I'm not stupid. Speak normally; if anything, speak extra fast. I get distracted easily because everyone in this world moves too slowly, and I get bored.

Of course, my thoughts were just my thoughts, and the nurse misread my confusion and joined in, speaking even more slowly than my new teacher.

"I think you will find that you'll feel better here. You'll fit in."

Fit in? Are you kidding me? I know she was trying to help but it only made it worse. As I looked around the room at my new peers I saw the kid who always had to wear that helmet with the chin strap. Next to him was the "retard" who was always drooling on himself. Yes, I know we can't say "retard" anymore. But back then that's how we talked, and it's important to understand what it meant to me at that moment, to be grouped with these kids. The rest of the class were the school bullies and trouble makers.

Is this me? Is this who I am? Is there where I belong?

I broke down and cried. I always knew I was different, but I liked me. And now, all of a sudden, I'm broken. I have a disorder, I have a deficit, and what is a deficit anyway? I'm dysfunctional, and apparently it's something I need to accept because it will probably be with me for the rest of my life.

Self-worth is a funny creature. It's a little animal inside of us living strong, and it will not hesitate to fight for its survival. Moreover, it will fight fiercely when we are young, but if it loses the fight at an early age it may never fight again. I went to that class for nearly a week. Every day I looked for and categorized all the reasons I didn't belong there—well, as best as a 5th grader can. It was more of an imaginary conversation I was having in my mind with my dad. I would play out what I was going to say, how he would react and what I might say next to get myself out of this class of misfits. I was almost ready for the big talk with my dad when something happened in class. I was talking with one of the other kids, explaining to him how I wanted to go back to my old class. I remember him looking at me with big eyes.

"Why?" he questioned.

My reply was simple.

"I just don't like it here."

Then he came back with the unarguable argument.

"But this class is so much easier!"

I don't remember much of my early years, but I remember that moment. I remember the struggle inside. A grand battle between the survival of the Self-Worth Creature and the Lazy Monster. I believe it was the first internal struggle of my young life. I was battling in my mind, truly wrestling for the first time with conflicting thoughts. My classmate was right, the class *was* easier—a lot easier. It was almost free time, all the time. Why would I want to go back to all the hard work, all the assignments with scores instead of a simple pass or incomplete? I enjoyed the rest of that day. It was fun. We played and goofed off. The teacher was so patient and expected so much less of us. By the time the final bell rang to go home, I thought, *I can stay here; this is easy.* The Self-Worth Creature was losing the fight to the Lazy Monster, my "natural man." I said nothing to my parents that night about wanting to leave the class. I thought maybe I should just stay "where I belong."

The next morning was a perfect day. I was in a good mood and excited to get to class. My twin brother, Mike, and I were walking to school the usual way, and I was bragging about how I didn't have as many books as he did to carry. I made the argument that he should try and get into my class as well. Being identical twins and all, he certainly had ADHD like me and could get the same deal I did. As we came around a corner, he listened intently to my argument for a easier way through school. But just when I thought I had him convinced, a screaming voice abruptly ended our conversation.

"Get off my damn lawn!"

We looked toward the voice to see a very angry (and unusually tall) Asian man, who I'll call Mr. Lee, coming our way with fists clenched. He continued toward us, one hand still a fist and the other now pointing at us.

"I've watched you two kids every morning cut the corner on my lawn and you've killed it! I've had enough of you stupid kids on my property!"

I didn't understand at the time where my rage came from, but something suddenly welled up inside me. I was boiling. I've always been taught to respect my elders, to respect property, to be polite and to take responsibly for my actions, but that all left me in a flash.

"I'M NOT STUPID!"

I made my hands into fists and turned to face him.

Mike kept walking.

"Come on, Mark; he's right, we shouldn't walk on his grass."

He pulled at my shirt sleeve to get me to follow, but I just shook my shoulder free and faced the man head on. The property owner was now only a few feet away and even angrier than before.

> "I STARED HIM DOWN FACE-TO-FACE, ALL 80 POUNDS OF ME READY TO FIGHT FOR THE HONOR OF MY INTELLIGENCE. OF COURSE, AT 80 POUNDS I WAS ONLY PROVING MY LACK OF INTELLIGENCE, OR AT LEAST, LACK OF GOOD JUDGEMENT."

"You talk to me like that again, boy . . . and I'll show you how stupid you are."

My personal Self-Worth Creature was now in full defense mode.

"I'm NOT stupid . . . you're stupid!"

It's funny how our comebacks as children aren't as clever sounding now as they sounded back then.

I stared him down (or up, really) face to face, all eighty pounds of me ready to fight for the honor of my intelligence. Of course, at eighty pounds I was only proving my lack of intelligence, or at least lack of good judgement. Mr. Lee glared back for some time, but when I was satisfied I had won the stare-down, I turned my back to him and muttered just loud enough for him to hear,

"You're the stupid one."

Just then I felt my neck crack as his fist hit me square in the back of the head. I hit the ground like it was pulled out from behind me. Face flat on the sidewalk, I wondered what hurt worse: my face from hitting the ground, or my neck from his punch. He walked back into his house and muttered back just loud enough for *me* to hear,

"Not feeling too smart now, are you? Stupid kid."

A little later, a policeman accompanied my father, Mike, and I to the property. The adults had an intense discussion before Mike and I were allowed to come over. Mike was such a good witness. This man was in trouble! When the police officer asked my dad if we wanted to press charges, my dad looked at Mike and me. "Well boys, is there something you need to say to Mr. Lee?" *What!? Um . . . what? Why is he asking us that? Press charges, Dad, this isn't about us!* My mind was racing. I could tell this was one of my dad's teaching moments, and I wanted nothing of it.

"No, DAD, he hit *me*!"

I was angry, but Dad remained as calm as usual as he continued.

"We will deal with him in a moment. Right now we are talking about you. You can never control who someone else will be, only who you are."

He paused long enough for us to think about what he was saying.

"Did you cut across his lawn?"

"Yes," I replied, "But . . ."

I could not even finish what I wanted to say. Dad interrupted.

"But nothing. We will deal with this one thing at a time. When you saw how upset he was about you cutting across his yard, did you apologize?"

Of course we hadn't apologized. I was too upset that he called us stupid. I knew my dad well enough to know that I would never get out of taking responsibility for my part of a conflict, and would have to own up to my actions regardless of what others had done. So I did the only thing I could. I turned to Mr. Lee and sincerely apologized. Mike did the same. My dad then asked Mr. Lee,

"Is there anything you wanted to say to my two sons?"

At first the man went on about his wife having just wrecked their only car, and the timing couldn't have been worse, but dad wasn't interested in that story. He looked at the cop and back at the man. "Is there something you wanted to say?" I thought the guy was going to cry. He gave the most humble and heartfelt apology I had ever heard, and even to this day I don't think I've heard a humbler man. No charges were pressed, but I can't say he got off without any consequences.

We went home and my dad asked why I reacted the way I did when Mr. Lee approached us on the lawn. I explained the only way I could, with a question.

"Dad, am I stupid?"

I remember his reaction. It was as if I had just broken his heart with those three simple words. And now I understand that I had. My dad is a therapist, as is my mom, and they teach courses on self-worth and the importance of it in youth. Nothing could devastate my dad like the awareness that one of his own kids was doubting their own value. He replied,

"Son, you are a child of God, with infinite worth."

He paused briefly and then continued.

"No. No, you are not stupid."

My dad has never lied to me, ever, so I believed him and suddenly, almost instantly, believed in myself again. Strengthened by his words, I asked the big follow-up question.

"Then why am I in a special class?"

I shudder to think what might have become of me if he responded with something like, "Because you're special." He didn't, and the next day I was back in my old class. I was not a "special needs" kid. Instead, I was challenged, and I faced my challenges head-on, much like I did with an unusually tall Asian man of recent acquaintance. I fought for my self-worth then, and I keep fighting for that fragile little creature today. Only now, I fight for all the little Self-Worth Creatures, within any of us, who have given up the fight. I fight with a firm belief that they never completely die inside any of us. Each just needs a reason to fight again. It needs to believe it's not broken, it doesn't have a deficit or a disorder; it's not dysfunctional. The Creature wants to be free to believe in itself again.

We are gifted, and we can be strong. Our ADHD minds are different—but again: *different is not a disorder*. We just need discipline and greater understanding, and for the little Self-Worth Creature inside to stand up and get back in the game.

A strong self-worth is quite possibly the single greatest key to success, and yet is so often destroyed at early ages. Give me any man, woman, or child with high self-worth, and I will give you a leader, a fighter, and a contributor to society regardless of their background, education, or upbringing. Give me anyone with self-doubt and I will show you someone only a step away from addiction and misbehavior that is seemingly beyond explanation.

"My prayer and my belief is that if the potential ADDers of the world wake up and learn what true greatness lies within, take responsibility for their actions, and learn to build on their ADHD gifts instead of looking at them as weaknesses, then true greatness can be achieved."

Most troubling to me is the fact that it is so much easier to destroy someone's self-worth than it is to build it up. Negative traits, beliefs, and habits are potentially much stronger than their positive counterparts. I don't understand exactly why, but it's the case with almost everything in life. Anything ignored is prone to decay, and if you're not consistently making an effort to improve yourself or your surroundings, it will all deteriorate. The "I can," neglected, will decay into the "I can't," and since our life here on earth is short, this is deeply concerning to me. My prayer and my belief is that if the ADDers of the world would wake up and learn what true greatness lies within, take responsibility for their actions, and learn to build on their ADHD gifts instead of viewing them as weaknesses, then true greatness would be achieved.

Our weaknesses must become our strengths, and with that strength we must help others. We will find success in what we do by the grace of God, and the gift of ADHD He has given us. And what a glorious gift it is. Magnify it, don't manage it. I have found my success *because* of my ADHD brain, not in spite of it. I'm so thankful for my Father in Heaven and the ADHD gift He has given me, and for my father on earth who has taught me that all gifts of God are meant to be magnified, not hidden. My commitment is to give all I have to lift another, and to teach them to do the same.

So, what are the Deadly Blows? They are the damage that come from anyone who does or says anything that will bring into question another's self-worth. The sad truth is, those delivering these blows often don't even know they're doing it. No parent or teacher wakes up in the morning and thinks, "What can I do to destroy the self-worth of a child today?" ADHD is real. It has unique challenges *and* powerful gifts, but without the self-belief required to manage that gift, it will only be a curse.

Give someone a healthy understanding of the potential advantages and disadvantages that come with ADHD, and you've given them the freedom and strength to grow. Give them a label, and you've given them an excuse. Self-worth grows in direct proportion to the amount of responsibility one takes for his or her own actions. An excuse, the label, will destroy that self-worth, the only thing absolutely required to achieve ultimate success.

YOUR GENIUS, AMPLIFIED!

The Three (maybe four) ADHD Ds

1. *Discard*
2. *Deflect*
3. *Decide*
(4. *Deny*)

Discard. If you're going to find success with ADHD, you must make a conscious choice to discard all the negative beliefs you've adopted as a result of living with the ADHD label. Throw them out on the street and lock the door, and no matter how often they try to creep back in (because they will), you must throw them out again.

Deflect. The world will continually point out the negatives of being ADHD, labeling you as stupid (deficit), broken (disorder), or dysfunctional, and you will need to deflect those deadly blows. You are not less than others. The attacks will come from all directions: a joke in a movie, a subtle comment from a friend or loved one, a new study or report on TV or in print. These blows will not stop, at least until we are able to change the world's perception of ADHD. Until then, keep your guard up and deflect each and every deadly blow. Dodge, duck, and let them glance or slide off you like water off a duck's back. Even if it's just in your own mind, defend yourself and your self-worth creature. There is no such thing as a little attack, each and every blow can be deadly. The second you buy into it, you are damned by your own beliefs and will become your own worst enemy.

Decide. Decide to focus on the positives. Decide to leverage your ADHD brain for better, not worse - you are married to it after all, and a divorce is out of the question. Decide to manage the curse, and magnify the gifts.

And, if necessary, *Denial.* If all else fails, and you can't accept that there might be anything good at all that comes with your ADHD brain, you could always try what I did. I lived in denial. Growing up, I stubbornly denied my ADHD, I deflected people's observations, comments, and questions about if I did, in fact, have Attention Deficit Hyperactivity Disorder. I found success in my deflection and denial. I was lying to myself more than anyone else, but it was easier for me to live in denial than to accept I was broken. And as unhealthy as that might seem, it worked. I lived in denial until I had enough successes to stop caring what others thought about my being ADHD. It didn't take long after that for me to not only accept my distracted brain, my ADHD, but to start seeing it for what it had always been for me - a gift.

> "What we are is God's gift to us.
>
> What we become is our gift to God."
>
> -Eleanor Powell

E.O. (Equal-Opposite) Comment by Dave Nielsen:

Self-worth is the lifeblood of both the ADDer and the E.O. As an E.O., don't do anything to destroy the self-worth of an ADDer. And be quick to defend him or her especially when he or she is not present.

I was in a high-level meeting with multiple companies, when an individual started criticizing his own C.E.O., who was not present. He described his boss as being distracted, late, always changing direction, etc. All of these adjectives told me his C.E.O. was more than likely an ADDer but unfortunately this executive didn't realize the great opportunity he had to work with such an individual, and that it was precisely because his C.E.O. was who he was that this criticizer had a job. Instead of becoming a great Equal-Opposite for his C.E.O., he was becoming his enemy and causing distrust, disloyalty, and possible implosion of the company from the inside.

Believe me, the benefits of getting to know, trust, and believe in the ADDers in your life will pay BIG dividends, reaching far beyond the boardroom.

-Dave

Deadly Blows TAKEAWAYS:

- ✓ Perspective is EVERYTHING!
- ✓ Self-Worth is possibly the single greatest key to success—don't allow negative ADHD stereotypes to impact yours.
- ✓ We often don't realize we're delivering Deadly Blows—be mindful of the labels we place on others.

Big Questions:

1. Have I unknowingly delivered any Deadly Blows?
2. Am I making a continual effort to improve?
3. Is my Self-worth Creature still fighting the good fight?
4. Who has been my "Mr. Lee"/ called me stupid? Did I believe it?

DISTRACTION:

In individuals with ADHD, as many as:
- 30 - 50% may be held back a grade.
- 35% quit school before graduating.
- 50% have serious social relationship issues.
- 25 -35% of teens with ADHD display anti-social behavior or "negative" conduct.

-chadd.org

Working together, we can bring those numbers down!

CHAPTER 4

THE ENTITLEMENT DISORDER

"When reward comes without effort, eventually the rewarded will want more than just their needs met. Their 'wants' will be relabeled as 'needs,' 'needs' will be presented as 'rights,' and their 'rights' will be demanded from others."

-Mark Patey

I met an interesting man who was originally from New Orleans, but who was now living on the streets of Kansas City, Missouri. I didn't meet him the way you would normally run into a homeless man—he wasn't begging for food, wasn't

looking for a handout, didn't hold up a sign with a clever plea for help. In fact, he was just walking down the sidewalk minding his own business. His old leather shoes were as worn out as his weather-beaten skin, and his down coat was flat in spots where all the feathers had fallen out of holes that were now duct taped shut. I've had mixed feelings about the homeless. Sometimes I see them with their signs and backpacks, and I'm angry. I catch myself thinking, "Get a job," as I drive or walk past. Yet other times I'll go out of my way to give them some cash to help out. I don't know why I feel different emotions at different times, but I've decided to trust my instincts. If my gut says give, I give liberally; if my gut says trouble, I walk on by. In this case, my heart instantly filled with compassion, so much so that at that moment I would have given this stranger anything he asked for. I wanted to understand him; I wanted to help him. I wanted to be a hand up to a man in obvious need, so I stopped him.

He seemed confused, and even nervous, that I engaged him in conversation, so I offered to buy him dinner. I thought some time with him would give us a chance to speak honestly and openly, thus giving me an opportunity to see how to best help out. With some trepidation, he agreed to come with me for a bite to eat.

I couldn't convince him to go anywhere fancy, which was probably a good thing as even the Denny's we ended up at didn't want to let him in until I firmly informed them that he was with me. After sitting down and reviewing the menu, the waitress asked for our order. I placed mine, and he sat, uncomfortable and quiet, for some time. I speculated to myself as to why he was so uneasy—maybe he was late for something, maybe he was carrying drugs, or maybe he just needed to use the bathroom. The waitress asked if she should come back and he replied,

"No, I'll just have some toast."

Confused, I asked, "Aren't you hungry?"

He nodded affirmatively but said again, "Toast will be fine."

I could tell he was obviously very hungry and wasn't going to order on his own, so I piped in, "And bring us your three most popular combo meals. The two of us will pick at whatever looks good."

The waitress agreed, then left. I tried to chit-chat the man, but he was slow to warm up. Finally, he looked me in the eyes and said something intriguing.

"I'm uncomfortable with you buying me dinner. I'm just so hungry . . . I had to accept."

I stopped sipping on my Diet Coke and swallowed hard as I tried to shake off the confused look on my face. "Why are you uncomfortable?" He looked down now, shaking his head a little as well.

"I didn't do anything to earn it."

You could have knocked me over with a feather. He didn't do anything to "EARN" it. This was nothing like most of the comments from other homeless folk and/or addicts I interviewed for this book. In fact, it was completely contrary. I've found that a common mentality shared by many addicts is a sense of entitlement. It's almost a disease in their thinking—

The Entitlement Disorder poster child. You go, Veruca.

an "Entitlement Disorder." They feel the world, the government, the rich, and even I, personally, owe them a living. I'd argue the Entitlement Disorder is why so many are trapped where they are. Once they have adopted the cancerous thinking that someone else is responsible for their needs, there is no drive or desire to work, to grow, to learn, or to progress, **only a need to hang out with a hand out** and wait. Some interviewed even expressed a "right" to take from those with more than them because "the rich don't deserve it." What a scary notion. When the discussion goes that way, and it often has with the addicts I've spoken to, I've always responded the same way:

"If they don't deserve what they have, what makes you think you deserve it?"

Honestly, it's a fruitless argument. Once they have the Entitlement Disorder there is no logic or reason, there is only a corrupted perception of reality: I *want*, therefore I *need*, therefore I have a *right* to it, and therefore, if it's not given to me, I'm *entitled* to *take* it.

What made this man so different? How could he be missing the Entitlement Disorder like so many of the addicts I'd interviewed? In response to his discomfort in my buying him dinner, I told him I needed some blessings in my own life, and therefore his allowing me to buy him dinner was helping me as much or more than it was helping him. His still uncomfortable look told me that didn't satisfy him. I took another stab at it. With a big, cheesy grin and a laugh in my voice I joked,

"You wouldn't rob me of the opportunity to earn some blessings in my own life, would you?"

With that he laughed, and relaxed. "No, I wouldn't want to rob you of that."

The meals came and the feast began. This man was packing it in: all three plates were consumed in a flash and the bread rolls were packed down into his coat pockets for consumption at a later time. As we chatted over dinner and then dessert, I noticed several things. First, he had an incredible vocabulary and perfect diction—obviously well-educated. Second, aside from the understandable volume of food consumed, his table manners were excellent. Third, he was thoughtful and engaging, as interested in me and my background as I was in him. Again, he was definitely a paradigm shift from the other interviewees.

Realizing dinner was wrapping up and I had not gotten to the bottom of who he was, I asked directly,

"How did you end up on the street?"

He looked at me for a bit and opened up. "Well, it wasn't drugs like you might think . . . "

Okay, I admit it. I try so hard not to profile, but it is hard to argue with the overwhelming statistics on the homeless and drug abuse. The thought had crossed my mind that he might be a drug addict. I smiled at him. "That's refreshing. So then, what was it? Loss of job . . ."

I paused to give him a chance to fill in the blank, and he did.

"I went crazy. I just kinda lost it."

He went on to explain that he was a teacher in New Orleans with good pay and benefits, was married once but that ended like many do, and that he had a high school-age son that he couldn't be more proud of. He told me that when his son died, though, he just fell apart and totally "lost it." His son was a star student. He'd avoided drugs and alcohol, got good grades, and was excited to go to college. He explained in length how proud he was of his son, and how few African-American boys from his neighborhood even finished high school, let alone went on to college. It was obvious there was a great deal of pain mixed with the pride he felt. When the timing was right, I asked what anyone would.

"How did your son die?"

He teared up a bit, looked me in the eyes, unashamed of his great pain, and replied,

"He was shot in the back, three times."

My heart broke. I didn't want to pry but in my shock at his answer I couldn't help myself.

"Why? What happened? Who did it?"

He then explained that his son had fallen in love with the wrong girl, and unfortunately, the girl loved him back. The problem wasn't love, it was the girl's ex-boyfriend who wanted her still. He was a known local drug dealer with a federal rap sheet longer than his education credentials, but hadn't done much time because, until recently, he was underage. I could hardly believe what I was hearing. I questioned further for clarification.

"Your son was shot in the back, three times, because a drug dealer wanted his girlfriend."

His explanation was chilling.

"You don't understand these kids. They feel they are entitled to whatever they want, and if you don't give it to them, they will take it anyway, at any cost to another. The kids these days, they don't know how to work, or what it means to earn something. They just take, take, take, and are never satisfied."

His son hadn't even known the drug dealer personally, just knew his girlfriend was scared to death of him. She had told him that this dealer said he would kill whoever tried to stop him from taking what was his. Unfortunately one evening, his son decided to confront the dealer. The shooting was on a public street in the girlfriend's neighborhood. There were witnesses, but nobody that was willing to testify for fear of their own life.

"Come on!" I blurted out finally, sitting up straight while throwing my arms back in frustration. I hated what I was hearing. My mind raced—this only happens in the movies, right? This doesn't happen in the real world. I continued out loud,

"Tell me he is in jail now . . ."

He looked at me sadly and shook his head no. The outer corners of his lips turned downward making a perfectly exaggerated upside-down U shape.

"You have got to be kidding me; they never arrested him?"

He again turned his lips down as he explained that he was taken in for questioning on several occasions, but no evidence, no willing witness, no conviction.

I hated this story so much I was starting to regret my choice to take him to dinner. Where was the justice? It's like a bad movie compounded with a sad ending. Life sucks! I wanted the Disney ending, or at least to just get home to my own life, my wife, and my four sons for a long hug. I sat quietly for a moment not knowing what else to say. I was in disbelief. I started talking again, but it was more of me just thinking out loud with him listening as I tried to reconcile all that was in my head.

"So, he just got off, scot-free?!! He's just hanging out with his friends, looking for another score?!!"

He shook his head no. I questioned instantly.

"He did or didn't get off scot-free?"

He clarified. "He didn't get caught for killing my son . . . but he isn't hanging out with his friends on the streets."

Finally, some hope. I leaned in looking for something—anything—redeeming to his story.

"Is he in jail for something else?"

41

His lips turned down even further, his eyes squinted in pain, causing wrinkles in that dark, leathery skin to reach from his eyes all the way back to his unkempt sideburns. The shaking of his head was so subtle it almost didn't move at all, yet it was clear he answered in the negative.

"Well, if he's not in jail, and he's not hanging out with his friends . . . where is he?"

"Dead."

It was a whisper, but deep in tone, like the word came up from his stomach. I looked around the room at everyone else enjoying their dinner with friends and family. They had no idea the gravity, the pain, the gut check that was going on over here at the corner table. I wasn't in Denny's like the rest of the patrons; I was completely sucked into this guy's life.

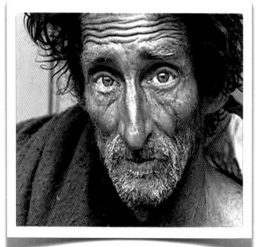

"How did he die?"

I had been bold in my questioning to this point; no reason to hold back the questions now.

"He was shot in the back . . ." a tear came down his cheek as he continued, " . . . three times."

I got goose bumps, and a sick feeling came over me.

I couldn't believe what I was experiencing. Did someone just confess a murder to me, a stranger in Denny's over pancakes and chicken-fried steak?

"Did you shoot him? Did you kill your son's killer?"

His reply was quick and full of anger; all pain left his face.

"No! Of course not!" He exclaimed.

He then went on and on about how the drug dealer always had his ex-girlfriend (yep, same one) with him every second of every day and how she always looked so sad and scared, and how he was once drunk and bragging at a party about getting away with the murder.

He went on for a while, and when he finally came up for air after his long story about what a bad guy the dealer was and how everyone knew he did it, I commented,

"If someone shot my son in the back, three times . . . I don't know how it would be possible to not go crazy, or lose it."

His defensive anger was gone as quickly as it came. His lips turned down, the wrinkles in his eyes returned with a now furrowed forehead. Tears flowing from both eyes, he said,

"Then you understand . . . as a father, you understand why I did it."

Internally, I was shocked. This man had reversed his earlier denial, and was now confessing to me that he had, in fact, killed his son's killer. Outwardly, I only nodded sympathetically as he continued.

"So now you know why I'm in Kansas City. Now you know why I'm homeless, why I can't ask for help from my friends or family."

It's strange, but it looked like, even felt like, a great load came off his shoulders as he confessed his past to me, a total stranger.

So, in writing about addicts and millionaires, why am I sharing this experience? I'm including it to point out my growing awareness of a disease afflicting our culture. A cancerous paradigm, not just in addicts and not just in our culture, but in a great number of people in countries all over the globe. It's what separates the addicts from the millionaires. The Entitlement Disorder. I had seen it in *all* of the addicts who were making no effort toward rehab, but I also saw this poisonous thinking, to some extent, in most of the other addicts I interviewed. I don't believe the Entitlement Disorder is the cause of addiction, but, rather, the reason they do not move away from the addiction. Once someone internalizes the idea that others are responsible for where they are, what they have, and/or where they are going in life, then there is no reason to make an effort of their own. The Entitlement Disorder is real: it corrupts the mind, damming its progression.

Nothing in life is free and nothing should be free. When reward comes without effort, eventually the rewarded will want more than just their needs met. Their "wants" will be relabeled as "needs," "needs" will be presented as "rights," and their "rights" will be demanded from others. In the end, they will demand for their wants and feel justified in any means to obtain them if others don't provide. And should those providing for their wants/needs/rights ever cease, the Entitled will take, even that which is not theirs. The Entitled may even take another person's life if it gives them what they want.

Life, liberty, and the pursuit of happiness? Life is a right, liberty is a right, and the *pursuit* of happiness is a right. Happiness itself, and everything else, is no one's right. When enough people feel justified in robbing the rights of one to fulfill another's wants/needs/rights, society will collapse under the weight of the ultimate addiction, entitlement. The Entitlement Disorder will stop any and all progress in any individual, group, state, or nation. You want to get off drugs? You have to do something about it. You want to be a millionaire? Earn it. You want happiness? Nobody is going to give it to you. Get off your butt, pick yourself up, and get to work, because nobody can or should do it for you.

Freedom from your addictions, whatever your addictions, is not free—it's earned.

When his confession was out on the table I was faced with an interesting dilemma. I understood why he took the drug dealer's life, but I also knew it was wrong. How ironic that he himself fell victim to the exact same Entitlement Disorder that disgusted him so much when he talked about the kids from this generation. A drug dealer *wanted* a girl, felt he *needed* the girl, deemed it his *right* to have the girl, and was thereby entitled to do whatever he had to in order to get the girl. Murder. A grieving father *wanted* the murderer to be held accountable for the murder, felt he *needed* to see justice, and thus deemed it his *right*, by any means, to exact justice. He felt entitled, perhaps only for a moment, to bring about justice, and he took the life of another to satisfy that sense of entitlement. **Wants are called needs, needs are relabeled as rights, rights become an entitlement, and then the end justifies the means.** Sadly, no law is enough to inhibit the actions of the entitled when their mental processes are so flawed.

But we do have laws and they must be obeyed. As much as I felt it would be a betrayal of trust, I was not his therapist (not legally anyway), and was in no way bound by client confidentiality. I am, as we all are, bound by the laws of the land we choose to live in. I knew I had to report him. I excused myself to the restroom to relieve myself from the pressure of the moment, as well as the pressure from an hour and a half of Diet Coke refills. When I came out of the restroom he was already gone. I'm sure he realized the seriousness of the confession, and before I had a chance to call the authorities, he was well on his way to the world he had hidden in for years. I can't help but wonder if his life on the street is his own personal prison, and could quite possibly be a greater punishment than a state prison where he would find three square meals a day, a warm bed, clean sheets, and clothing.

The reality is this: We all live in the prisons we create for ourselves. The moment we deceive ourselves into believing that our wants are rights to be demanded from others, we have forever locked ourselves into a prison: the forever-damning bars of the Entitlement Disorder.

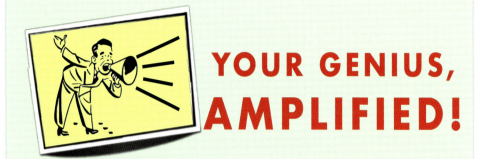

YOUR GENIUS, AMPLIFIED!

The ADHD Three Es:

1. Entitlement

2. Escape

3. Earning It

Entitlement. Entitlement is a mental disorder and should be seen as the greatest roadblock to anyone's personal progress. Yep, I said that. Free speech practiced here.

Escape. Escape the temptation to buy into the lie that you have a right to special privileges simply because you were born different, born with ADHD. Escape the trap of thinking you have permission or a right to misbehave, act out, be forgetful, be late, fail to complete a task, overreact, or in any way perform below your potential. Escape the Entitlement Disorder.

Earning It. You have abilities, talents, skills, even gifts that make it possible to achieve greatness. All that's left is the work required to earn it. If you think you're without skills, well, even skills are earned. Expect nothing for free–earn it. Expect nothing to come easy–earn it. Ask for no handouts or special privileges. Success is earned, respect is earned, wealth is earned, love is earned, even happiness is earned, and it's all earned over time. Get to work–no excuses. Show me an excuse maker, and I'll show you someone guaranteed to amount to jack squat (edited for content).

"Inspiration exists, but it has to find us working."
-Pablo Picasso

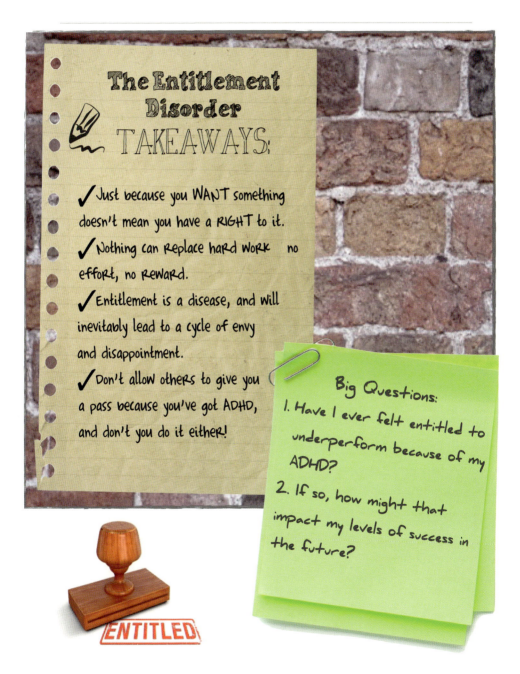

The Entitlement Disorder TAKEAWAYS:

- ✓ Just because you WANT something doesn't mean you have a RIGHT to it.
- ✓ Nothing can Replace haRd woRk   no effoRt, no RewaRd.
- ✓ Entitlement is a disease, and will inevitably lead to a cycle of envy and disappointment.
- ✓ Don't allow otheRs to give you a pass because you've got ADHD, and don't you do it eitheR!

Big Questions:
1. Have I ever felt entitled to underperform because of my ADHD?
2. If so, how might that impact my levels of success in the future?

"A lot of parents today are terrified that something they say to their children might make them 'feel bad.' But, hey, if they've done something wrong, they should feel bad. Kids with a sense of responsibility, not entitlement, who know when to experience gratitude and humility, will be better at navigating the social shoals of college."

- Amy Chua

"Man is not, by nature, deserving of all that he wants. When we think that we are automatically entitled to something, that is when we start walking all over others to get it."

-Criss Jami

"Instead of communicating 'I love you, so let me make life easy for you,' I decided that my message needed to be something more along these lines: 'I love you. I believe in you. I know what you're capable of. So I'm going to make you work.'"

-Kay Wills Wyma, *Cleaning House: A Mom's Twelve-Month Experiment to Rid Her Home of Youth Entitlement*

"You have to do your own growing, no matter how tall your grandfather was."

- Abraham Lincoln

"It is easy, when you are young, to believe that what you desire is no less than what you deserve, to assume that if you want something badly enough, it is your God-given right to have it."

-Jon Krakauer, *Into the Wild*

"Entitlement is the opposite of enchantment."

- Guy Kawasaki

CHAPTER 5

BEST IDEA EVER!

"Good ideas are common—what's uncommon are people who'll work hard enough to bring them about."

~ Ashleigh Brilliant

I was driving down Utah's I-15 last week when my mind triggered on something spectacular. The next thirty minutes was a complete brain blast, like the cartoon with Jimmy Neutron when his mind is firing on all receptors to create something or solve a problem. (Disclaimer: I have kids and I like watching cartoons with them. To be honest, sometimes my kids don't even need to be there.) This particular brain blast was the Best Idea Ever. It could change the world! I was going to be richer than Richie Rich (cartoon reference for those who grew up in the 80s). The only problem with the idea was . . . well, nothing, it was perfect—other than I can't remember what it was. (#!@*$!)

> **DISTRACTION:**
> More electrical impulses are generated in one day by a single human brain than by all the telephones in the **world.**

Make sure that when a Best Idea Ever pops into your head you write it down, or call your Equal-Opposite right away to discuss it. More often than not, good ideas for an ADDer leave as fast as they come. Sometimes ideas or solutions to problems come in the middle of the night, waking you without warning. Have a pen and paper ready at your bedside. This is not unique to those of us blessed with ADHD, however it seems to be much more common in the ADDers than it is in the "Normals." NOTE: ADDicts don't generally make good records of their ideas for further examination; ADDers do.

One of the gifts of the ADHD brain is the ability to create on the fly, both consciously *and* subconsciously. Understand that when the creative subconscious solves a problem, it will present the solution or idea to the conscious mind without warning. You are then left to deal with all aspects of the new concept on a conscious level even if the timing is bad, like when you're trying to sleep or are otherwise engaged in "more important" things.

I was sitting in a board meeting with a few business partners and investors for one of our companies. The items at hand were of significant importance and required my attention and my particular skill set. Without warning, my creative subconscious, that busy little genius inside (I call him Trigger), threw me a solution to a different problem he'd been working on without me, or at least he'd been working on it without my conscious mind. Since installing a new, larger motor in my race plane, I had been having troubles with overheating turbos. Now, suddenly, in the middle of the board meeting, Trigger is jumping in, interrupting me (without my permission, I might add), to enthusiastically share with me the solutions to my turbo problems. (Distraction: This sounds like a multiple personality disorder, I know, but it's just a creative way to explain how the mind works . . . or is it? I was going to write a book on solving multiple personality disorders, but Trigger and I couldn't decide who would get the credit.) Instantly, I was "distracted" in the board meeting. I was on a new path of my own, brainstorming on how I could change in a significant

Mark with one of his ideas.

manner the way my plane handled fuel flows, ignition timing advance, turbo boost controllers, and inlet air temperatures to bring down my high turbo temps. These modifications would allow me to run higher manifold pressures and power settings with less risk of engine failure, ultimately resulting in more speed and safety for an upcoming race. This was all very exciting stuff for a competitive aviation addict like myself. However, where was Mark Patey? Physically, I was in a board room with my peers, but mentally, I'm welding a new exhaust manifold, advancing my ignition timing, and winning my next big race in Texas with a calculated 3.2 knots higher airspeed. The board members need me in the board room and I'm in my cockpit flying at full power headed for a checkered flag. Yahoo!!! Funny how things trigger in our minds, or in other words, how Trigger is working in our minds at all times to create and solve whatever problems we placed in our subconscious.

Dave Nielson, my Equal-Opposite, has become an expert at seeing this creative leap in me. He knows when Trigger happens. Noticing my eyes had glazed over during the financial portion of the board meeting, Dave leaned over to me and simply whispered, "Mark, is there anything you want me to write down for future review or discussion?" He didn't say, "Hey, you dipwad, pay attention!" or anything like that. He knows that my "distractions" are usually productive, just not always for the task at hand. Many will see the "distraction" and be bothered or even angry. They might lose confidence in the ADDer, which could cost the ADDer his/her job, good grade, marriage . . . who knows what else? However, a good Equal-Opposite will recognize the creative leaps as part of the ADHD gift. Sure, it can be a challenge, but like anything in life, it's a "give and take" and well worth the investment in helping the ADDer learn to put that gift to good use. Instead of trying to shut down the ADHD traits, we should strive to learn how to recognize the gift and leverage it for good.

As ADDers, we must learn to watch vigilantly where our mind is going, and why it's going there. Track its every move. Don't let it run off on its own, but DEFINITELY don't shut it down, either. Put it to work. Give it a chance to take the Best Idea Ever and make something of it. The Normals will have you try and fix or *manage* your ADHD brain. I say *magnify* it! Leverage it! Engage it at every opportunity! Challenge it. It is a muscle, after all—give it a workout. Don't self-medicate it to sleep with drugs, alcohol, video games, or other addictions, but rather let that creative subconscious genius inside you make you successful, happy, and even wealthy, if that's important to you. Think of your ADHD mind as if it were the greatest gift given to man. Only seven in one hundred people get that gift, and only a small percentage of that seven learn to leverage it. It's like you've won Mother Nature's greatest lottery, and if you don't invest your winnings into worthwhile endeavors, you will lose them. That would be like those idiots that win an actual lottery and then waste every dime of it doing pointless things. Don't be that person; don't sell yourself short. The vast majority of the millionaires studied and interviewed for this book fully believe that their successes came about largely as a direct result of that ADHD gift, not in spite of it. The ADDicts were too busy placing blame on the very gift that could have, and still could, make them successful. You choose—Addict or Millionaire, ADDict or ADDer. The beauty of it all is that it doesn't matter where you are today. The creative genius you were born with is still inside you, and Trigger's dying to come out and play.

YOUR GENIUS, AMPLIFIED!

You have an amazing brain. Use it!

Best Idea Ever!
TAKEAWAYS:

- ✓ Don't shut down the ADHD brain—challenge it!
- ✓ Discuss ideas with an E.O.
- ✓ Let Trigger run free every now and again. He could use the exercise.
- ✓ E.O.s help ADDers recognize and leverage the gift.
- ✓ "Every truly great invention was once someone's distraction."
  —Mark Patey

Big Questions:

1. Have I ever had a great idea and lost it? (Arrrgh!)
2. Where might I be today if I had embraced the distractions?
3. Do I make an effort at all times to track where my ADHD brain is going, or do I let it wander aimlessly off on its own?

E.O. Comment:

There I was, enjoying sushi with a friend when my phone rang. I checked the caller i.d.-Mark Patey. I was fully engaged in a great conversation and salivating for my next bite of the BSCR roll, but I didn't even hesitate. As I moved to answer, my friend asked, "Can't that wait?" My immediate response was, "Absolutely not. It could be another million-dollar idea from Mark!" Equal-Opposites need to be excited rather than annoyed when the ADDer calls at unusual hours or inconvenient times. I'm not talking about giving them carte-blanche to take over your life; just understand that inspiration doesn't always happen during business hours.

Additionally, suppose you're in an important meeting, or trying to get your point across to your ADDer and he seems distant or unresponsive. Often, when an ADDer seems distracted it's because he's pondering a problem or having a stroke of creativity for another venture. Relax, and again, don't be annoyed, be excited.

And ADDers, answer your phone when your Equal-Opposite calls you! If they are a good E.O., they are typically calling for your benefit, not theirs— perhaps a reminder for an important meeting or phone call. So pick up, please! (Mark, this is in no way directed at you . . .)

-Dave

CHAPTER 6

THE REALITY FOG

"The best way to predict the future is to invent it."

~ John Scully, 1987

Have you ever noticed that superheroes almost always have gifts *and* curses? The two seem to go hand in hand. The Hulk has incredible strength, but he's a raging monster when he uses it. The X-Men all have awesome powers, but those powers brand them as outcasts. Spider Man can climb walls, but he can't take any public credit for his amazing deeds.

The same holds true for ADHD. As we're talking about the gifts and curses of ADHD, one curse I've found to be most frustrating and challenging is what I call The Reality Fog. It actually stems from the creative gifts in ADDers. Specifically, it is the creative mind of an ADDer filling in the blanks from past experiences with knowledge of questionable accuracy, or what it may perceive as knowledge/facts. The problem is that it's not always accurate. In fact, as a result of the hyper-creative ADDer mind, the "facts" can be outright ridiculous. Yet we accept it as truth.

There is a fog between what really happened, and what we *believe* happened. My little brother, Dave, a gifted ADDer, after telling a funny or amazing story, will say with a big, cheesy grin, "You think that was a good story now, just wait for a few years—it'll be awesome . . . my stories get so much better with time!" It is not his or any ADDer's, intent to embellish or distort the facts, nor to deceive anyone. Actually, it's often the desire to tell the truth that creates this problem.

Here's what happens: over time, memories fade for everyone. It's just the way it is, and it is inescapable. However, the ADHD mind is a problem-solving mind; it *must make sense of things it doesn't understand*, it *must finish things*, it *has to fill in the blanks*. For Normals, as memories fade, they will tell the event and simply leave out what

> "OUR MINDS CAN CREATE A 'REALITY' AS FAST AS OUR LIPS MOVE, AND SADLY, WE WILL BELIEVE IT."

they've forgotten. No big deal. ADDers, however, find it almost impossible to leave a blank. So we fill it in on the fly, and usually without any conscious thought or effort. Our minds can create a "reality" as fast as our lips move, and sadly, we will believe it. The human brain doesn't discern very well between memories created and memories lived: they are all just memories. So, in the event that a hyper-creative brain is faced with empty holes or foggy memories, it will fill in missing information, resulting in The Reality Fog.

To better understand how this happens, it's important to understand how the brain works. One of the greatest gifts of the human mind is its ability to fill in gaps. This innate and uniquely human trait allows us to anticipate and—when needed—make decisions without all the "necessary" information. The following article describes how the mind does this with what it sees, hears, and feels.

WHAT YOUR EYES CAN'T SEE THE BRAIN FILLS IN
(PhysOrg.com, 04/2011)

Researchers from the University of Glasgow have shown that when parts of our vision are blocked, the brain steps in to fill in the blanks.

The team from the Institute of Neuroscience and Psychology conducted a series of experiments that showed how our brains predict what cannot be seen **by drawing on our previous experiences to build up an accurate picture.**

The results show that our brains do not rely solely on what is shown to the eyes in order to 'see'. Instead the brain constructs a complex prediction.

Dr. Lars Muckli, from the University's Institute of Neuroscience and Psychology said, **"We are continuously anticipating what we will see, hear, or feel next.** *If parts of an image are obstructed we still have a precise expectation of what the whole object will look like.*

"When direct input from the eye is obstructed, the brain still predicts what is likely to be present behind the object by using some of the other inputs to come up with best 'guesses'.

The Wright Brothers

Albert Einstein

Thomas Edison

"Embrace that crazy." -Mark Patey

> **"EFFECTIVELY, OUR BRAINS CONSTRUCT AN INCREDIBLY COMPLEX JIGSAW PUZZLE USING ANY PIECES IT CAN GET ACCESS TO."**

"We showed three different images to a group of subjects. The lower right section of each image was covered with a white rectangle. Using MRI brain imaging equipment we then measured brain activity in the region responding to the white rectangle."

Dr. Fraser Smith, from the same institute, said: "On first sight, the brain's response to the white rectangle is quite similar for each image but we were able to use brain reading techniques to reveal what the subject's brain 'saw' behind the white panel. Subjects don't see what is hidden but the brain is still able to make a good estimate.

"Effectively, our brains construct an incredibly complex jigsaw puzzle using any pieces it can get access to. These are provided by the context in which we see them, our memories, and our other senses."

Dr. Muckli added: "Sometimes the brain's guess can be so convincing that we see visual illusions; in our example there was no visual illusion seen – the white space was not filled-in by an actual illusion. Nevertheless, we found a way to reveal the brain's guess of what lies behind the object."

Dr. Muckli's statement, "We are continuously anticipating what we will see, hear, or feel next," is notable. It's not only what we see; our minds will also fill in the gaps for what we "hear" and even what we might "feel." I would propose the brain does the same for every form of input—sight, sound, smell, taste, touch, and it even fills in the gaps in our memories. The reason this is especially true for a person with ADHD is because of the incredible speed at which the ADHD brain can create: It often "sees" ten levels deep, and in ten different directions at once. It is a multitasking muscle machine that operates at blinding speeds. It's faster than a speeding bullet, more powerful than a locomotive, capable of leaping tall buildings in a single bound.

Unfortunately, without proper awareness and discipline, it will do all of the above without the express written consent of your conscious mind.

Gifts and Curses of The Reality Fog

The Gifts:

1. ADDers are great forecasters.
2. They see problems others do not.
3. They can quickly provide multiple possible solutions or scenarios for any given circumstance.
4. They can see beyond the obvious and can quickly fill in holes.

One of humankind's most valuable assets is its ability to **forecast**, **problem solve**, and **predict potential outcomes**, both positive and negative. The ADHD mind is uniquely gifted in that regard. It will see the "fog" in life and it will work with incredible efficiency to clear it up. ADHD inventors see a need and fill it, see a problem and fix it, and are usually successful because they see what nobody else can. Interestingly, history has taught us that many of our greatest inventors were ADDers. Thomas Edison, the Wright Brothers, Alexander Graham Bell, Benjamin Franklin, and Albert Einstein, to name a few, were all ADHD, and gifted as a result of their ADHD brains—not in spite of them.

Have you ever noticed that if an ADDer is rich, they call him eccentric, but if he is poor they just call him crazy? I suggest that almost every ADDer with a truly out-of-the-box idea was called crazy at first, and only seen for the genius they were *after* the results were brought to light. Keep in mind . . . you don't have to be crazy to be successful, BUT IT SURE HELPS!

The Curses:

1. Difficulty discerning reality vs. reality fog.
2. Others may see them as dishonest.
3. Can be tempted to use their creative gifts to fabricate fiction.

An agreement I have with my four sons is that as long as I pay for their cell phones, I have a right to read their text messages. So, if they don't want me reading it, they shouldn't text it. And if they aren't texting it because I would be disappointed in reading it, then maybe they should rethink their topics of conversation. Well, on one occasion my ADHD teenager was texting at 1:00 a.m. on a school night. When caught, we asked for his phone immediately and grounded him from it for breaking school-night texting rules, and like most concerned parents might, we reviewed his texting history. My wife, Suzy, and I were disappointed to see that he

had been going on and on telling a story that was mostly fabricated in an attempt to help a girl who was struggling with depression. We were pleased with his noble efforts to help this young lady, but why the lies or half-truths? When we asked him why he'd been making up parts of his stories, he simply replied, "I don't know. I know I shouldn't have; it was just easier." There are several interesting things about his comment. The first is the fact that the truth in its entirety would have been a better story; he had nothing to gain by fabricating at all. He could create on the fly, and he did it because it was easy.

Writers can only dream of creating as quickly and effortlessly the things that were flowing from his fingertips. The challenge is to not use a creative gift for evil. Sounds funny, I know, but as I've mentioned in my other writings I believe the ADHD brain is a gift, like a super power, and we must use if for good. Evil is too easy. We must force ourselves to watch fervently where our minds are going and why. Am I creating to benefit and problem-solve, or am I just creating because I'm so good at it and I have nothing better to do? I often feel as if my ADHD brain is like a child: it brings me more joy and happiness than anyone could ever understand, but I have to keep an eye on it 24/7 or it will wander off, running its own show.

> *"If you tell the truth, you don't have to remember anything."*
> *-Mark Twain*

Reality is a funny thing. Time erases it, perceptions skew it, the ADHD brain can recreate it in a blink, and history is in the eye of the beholder. So who really knows what truth is, in the end? This is why it is so important for us ADDers to keep vigilant. We need to stay focused, always watch our thoughts, and track where they are going. We have to ask ourselves, "Am I remembering, or creating?" Only in that constant questioning can we avoid the curses of the Reality Fog. However, and equally important, we must remember the gifts that come with the ADHD brain's ability to create.

What's real and possible to one is unrealistic and impossible to another. I would argue the realm of the unrealistic and impossible, is where the ADHD brain thrives. It longs to solve problems, to create solutions, to invent, to discover, and to grow. Yet if left on its own it will stray, and that's rarely a good thing. In the end, reality is what we make of it. Make sure you are making something productive and for the good of all humankind. After all, you're pretty much a superhero, and "whom unto much is given, much is required."

DiSTRACTiON:
An ADHD Awareness Coalition Survey found that
- 60% of adults with ADHD attributed a lost or changed job to his/her ADHD symptoms.
- 36% had 4 or more jobs in ten years.
- 6.5% had 10 or more jobs in the past 10 years.

YOUR GENIUS, AMPLIFIED!

The ADHD Three Rs

1. Risks

2. Reality

3. Rewards

Risks. The greatest risk of allowing a reality fog to build in your mind is a eventual and inevitable loss of identity-a reality fog of who you really are. The outcome is a swaying in your own beliefs and convictions; who you are, what you stand for, and what matters most in your life are all in jeopardy. The eventual outcomes are often the same: life paths you never wanted and a deep and devastating depression.

Reality. The reality is this: avoiding the Reality Fog takes an honest, full-time effort. Filling in the blanks with creative creations is easy (why do you think we are so quick-witted?), but holding back and digging through our memories in a honest search for truth takes work. Earn a great memory, filled only with truth, by exercising your brain looking for truth.

Rewards. The rewards of a commitment to truth in all things shouldn't have to be spelled out here but lets do it any way: a greater sense of high self-worth, trust among your peers, and confidence in daily conversation, to name only a few. On top of all that, the rewards that come from magnifying the gifts of the ADHD brain are far greater than any false sense of reality one could create in the mind.

The Reality Fog
TAKEAWAYS:

✓ ADDers have a need to fill in the blanks, and if we're not careful, we create a dangerous "Reality Fog."

✓ It's true reality is what we make it, so make it true.

✓ Commit to being completely honest, recognizing that a lie is only communication given with the intent to deceive.

✓ Embrace that crazy!

Big Questions:
1. Is the reality I present real or created?
2. If created, what led me to do that?
3. How might a Reality Fog prevent me from reaching my goals?

CHAPTER 7

CREATIVITY AMPLIFIED

*"Creativity is born from chaos.
You can't remove one without
risking the existence of the other"*

~ Mark Patey

I've always felt there was a happy little fat kid inside me dying to get out . . . I just don't feed him. The opposite can be said, too: there's a buff beach body inside me dying to get out . . . I just feed him too much. I believe the ADHD gift is the same. There is a creative, spontaneous, energetic, problem-solving little genius inside of all of us, dying to be set free. We just aren't feeding it. In fact, the opposite is true: we are starving it. Our culture is so determined to get people to fall in line, to prescribe some sort of "normal," that we teach with such a well-defined, rigid curriculum, that any deviation is seen as unacceptable, and even labeled as dysfunctional. Well, let's be a little dysfunctional then, shall we?

Let's let that child within off its chain, unbolt the door, and lead it out into the the world to discover, to question everything, learn, grow, make mistakes, and recover from them. What's the risk? A bruised knee, a little embarrassment at an odd or quirky behavior or two? **Who CARES?** Let loose.

Be a kid again. Set yourself free from the confines of the "norm." **RELAX!** My oh-so-wise mother would always say, "Go have fun . . . as long as it's not illegal, immoral, or fattening!" And I agree—why not have some fun?! Of course, her "fattening" comment was not really the point, it was just her funny way of saying as long as it's not unhealthy (i.e. potentially deadly.) Certainly ADDictive behaviors fit into all three of those categories.

Creativity is such a fun thing to work with, because the secret to it is that it requires no work. In fact, the harder you work at being creative the less creative you will be. It is something that flows from within you. It is not a conscious process, but rather an instinctual one. Our entire lives we are taught to process, think through, list, categorize, label, define, and put into order everything we come in contact with. The art of creativity is the opposite. It is letting go, abandoning conscious thought, silencing the restrictive world of the organized mind. It's more truthfully said that if you are *trying* to think creatively, certainly it will not be creative.

A slightly overprotective mother means goodbye social life.

When you want something creative to come from your mouth, open it and speak without preparation. If you want something creative on a canvas, make the first stroke with your brush without having decided what it will become. It's risky, but oh, so much fun. Creativity is a leap of faith, but more often than not, what comes out of your mouth and what shows up on your canvas will surprise you in its simple ingenuity. ADDers are always being told to "look before you leap, think before you speak lest you jump into a pile of trouble, or open you mouth and prove yourself an idiot." Well, I'm here to tell you that it is impossible to have it both ways. Creativity is born from chaos. You can't remove one without risking the existence of the other.

If we lived in a world without risk, we would live in a very boring place. No cars, no planes, no bikes, no rock climbing, nothing . . . just a world of people trying to protect other people from themselves. But guess what? It's not possible to remove the risk from life and all things in it. The one guarantee we all get in this life is our inevitable death. To live is to assure death, but to live without risk is a fate worse than death itself.

How often do you hear someone complain that they had the very idea someone else made a million dollars with? It's a sad and common story. It always starts with, "I thought of that idea years ago, but I just didn't pursue it, and now *that* guy is a multi-millionaire." Boo hoo. The only difference between you and the hundred other people that thought of that idea, and the guy that made something of it, was a willingness to risk. Don't hate him for it, you're the one that played it safe. No risk, no _____. (You fill in the blank.) So it is with all things creative. Take the first step and start, even if you don't know what you are going to start yet. Just sit down with a piece of paper, a pen, and MOST IMPORTANTLY an empty mind (that part is easy for me.) Then start writing without thinking about it; don't let your pen stop. You may get half a sentence on the paper and still not know where your creative mind is going with it. In fact, you might write several sentences down before you understand where you're

"It is in the character of very few men to honor without envy a friend who has prospered."
-Aeschylus

headed. It's important to not allow the supposedly superior conscious mind to take over; it's not that creative, and far too organized to be capable of abstract thought. It will only get in the way and rob you of a fantastic learning experience. **I firmly believe our creative subconscious is far wiser than our conscious mind.** The conscious mind can only handle so much data at one time; it's like a computer with limited RAM. The creative subconscious is a big fat hard drive that's capable of storing a lifetime's worth of memories, thoughts, beliefs, and all manner of random tidbits of information. That creative subconscious is a freaking genius, we just don't listen to it often enough.

Like I mentioned in the last chapter, there's a reason people say, "You don't have to be crazy to be successful, but it helps." Like most things we find funny, it's based in truth. Successful people are often seen as a little crazy. That's why we have the term "eccentric millionaire." (Distraction: An old joke: Do you know the difference between a crazy man and an eccentric millionaire? Only the size of their wallet.) The "crazy" reference is what we're trying to avoid. You never know what the "creative you" will want to talk about. It's like the ADHD personality: it just jumps around from one random thing to another. But watch it long enough, listen long enough, and we will find an entirely new tool for solving life's little problems. I say "little problems," because all problems are little if you have the right perspective. **A problem is the catalyst to the birth of its own solution.** You have the solution to every problem within yourself if you will just listen to the creative and instinctive genius inside you.

As a child I was blessed and cursed, as most kids with ADHD are, in that I functioned mostly off of that creative subconscious mind. I let it run rampant, controlling my actions, leaping before looking, speaking before thinking, and creating all manner of trouble. Now, I know what you're thinking. "But Mark, I understood you earlier to mean that we need to let that part of our minds free—let it outside to play. Right?" Yes, you're right, I'm actually saying two things that appear to conflict. But stick with me for a minute. This is why the multitasking gift found in all ADDers is so important. You need to learn to listen to the "creative you" on the subconscious level at the same time you are processing everything else on a conscious level. Sounds almost like having multiple personalities, but it's not even close. It's learning to use two different parts of your brain at the same time, the left and right sides working together simultaneously. Let your conscious mind filter what's coming from your creative subconscious *without* shutting off the subconscious. Filter, don't dismantle. I've read so many articles and books on how to manage ADHD, and what they are really doing is teaching you to turn it off. I say magnify your ADHD gifts and become a true ADDer; magnify it like you magnify something with a looking glass. Learn to really look at it closely—monitor it for the genius it has to offer. Don't manage it into nonexistence.

For those who want to awaken the ADHD gift, you need to practice listening to that creative instinct. The above-mentioned pen, paper, and empty mind exercise is a great way to get started. For someone with ADHD who wants to make sure they become an ADDer and not and ADDict, they need to learn to filter what's coming from that wonderful, hyperactive brain without *ever* muting it or turning it off. Our ADHD brains are our greatest gift—shut it down and I believe you are destroying in large part what makes you who you are: a truly great, talented, and creative genius.

Creativity Amplified
TAKEAWAYS:

✓ It's okay to deviate from the norm.
✓ Don't force creativity—let it happen.
✓ Learn to listen to the creative you.
✓ Allow the occasional distraction, and pursue it if time permits.
✓ There is a solution to every problem if you allow true creativity. An overly-structured mind may never think abstractly enough to see it.

Big Questions

1. What have I risked by over-managing my ADHD brain?
2. How can I build an environment that allows me to be creative?

CHAPTER 8

DISTRACTIONS VS. OPPORTUNITIES

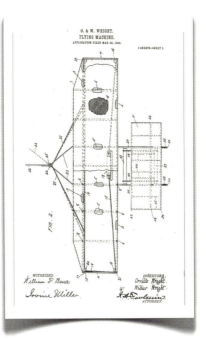

There are a million ways to make a million bucks - pick one, or two . . . but no more than three. ;) The millionaire ADDers interviewed for this book ALL had several things on their plate at the same time—multiple businesses, future business plans, and new ideas brewing in the mental incubator. Never did they have only one thing going, and that's to be expected with an ADDer. However, for the most part they all had a similar system, a "controlled chaos" if you will, that kept things moving forward in a productive way. The ADDicts I interviewed had an idea per minute (just like the ADDers), but there was no control to the chaos—just chaos. They were constantly jumping from one idea to the next without ever finishing the first. Even in the interview process, the ADDicts were laying out business ideas for me to consider investing in. Some of the ideas were actually good ideas, but the problem with investing in a good idea from an ADDict, aside from the obvious addiction problems, is I could tell the ideas would likely never be more than just that—good ideas. I did find it rather humorous that the blind optimism I love in the ADHD personality was still alive in the ADDicts. One of the ADDicts I interviewed was in prison, and was still excited to share his business plan with me as if I was going to invest that very day.

All I could do was grin like an idiot and laugh inside, not at his naivety, but at his optimism. I loved it. I didn't invest, but I loved it. Certainly, blind optimism is one of the gifts and curses of ADHD. You could say the Wright Brothers were gifted with a blind, even unquenchable, optimism to believe that they, as bike builders, could build an airplane. What a gift to be so blind to the "reality" that powered flight was unachievable.

As I write today, I'm sitting in the parking lot of the Riverside Country Club. The RCC is *the* place for lunch and a game of golf if you are, or want to pretend to be, one of the "elite" in Utah County. I'm here for an important business meeting because a fun project is quickly turning into a huge business opportunity. In fact, an offer is on the table that could put nearly six million dollars in the bank (after all expenses) in the next twelve months. Exciting? Yes. But is it just another distraction, or is it an opportunity? Often, it's both. The problem is that I know my ADHD self all too well, and my time and other commitments and goals will suffer if I make this deal. With everything currently on my plate, it would certainly take away from my abilities to achieve other goals, specifically my desire to make a difference in the world. The one goal, of course, that's closest to my heart is finishing this book. What an interesting challenge: I'm writing a book on ADHD and I can't seem to finish it because I keep getting distracted . . .

So what do we, as ADDers, do when yet another opportunity presents itself?

First, recognize that not all opportunities need to be pursued. As an ADDer, you will find you have a strong, almost uncontrollable desire to achieve or pursue whatever new goal or idea pops into your head. In fact, the desire to complete a new goal will almost certainly outweigh your previous Best Idea Ever, goal, or business plan. I have a brother that says he is a serial entrepreneur. That's one way to describe it. I call it "the ADHD gift and curse at its best and worst." He consistently bounces from one new business idea to the next. It can be quite frustrating to work with him because the changes in business direction seem to come daily, sometimes even hourly, and on his particularly creative days he can change business directions three times in a one hour board meeting. Moreover, just when everyone thinks they have a handle on how to run the business around him, he changes it again, or just sells the company without warning and moves to the next Best Idea Ever. The gift my brother has is the very thing that frustrates everyone. Any business that is not flexible is destined for failure. You will never find an example of a successful company that laid out a business plan and followed flawlessly. Business is a constantly moving target, with unforeseen obstacles and pitfalls to be avoided in an ever-changing marketplace. **The reason you find so many millionaires and billionaires with ADHD is because that creative, turn-on-a-dime brain is necessary to navigate an uncertain landscape**. However, that gift can easily become a curse without an Equal-Opposite around to help flesh out and make sure the Best-Idea-Ever isn't just another distraction but is, in fact, an opportunity. Which leads me to . . .

The Equal-Opposite: it's like having your own personal superhero.

Second, consult your Equal-Opposite. Every millionaire ADDer I interviewed for this book had at least one Equal-Opposite, and in most cases had several: an Equal-Opposite in each critical part of their life or business. This is not by chance. It is not just an interesting phenomenon that the most successful ADDers in the world have Equal-Opposites. I believe it's a simple fact that our minds are different and have different talents and purposes in Mother Nature's grand scheme of things. We ADDers are wired, if you will, to create, to think way outside the proverbial box. Normals are wired to put order to things, to bring logic and reason, to put things in their proper place and balance. If our ADHD minds were wired that way, we would not be capable of the abstract thought we are so gifted with. Don't try to be both! Discuss your thoughts with a good Equal-Opposite, and in doing so you will find that as they present questions and challenges to your ideas, your problem-solving mind will then flesh out solutions. Recognize this question-answer process as their role, their purpose in being there. I see too many gifted ADDers that get frustrated with a Normal who says, "You can't do that," or "That's kind of a lofty goal, isn't it?"

Don't get frustrated. **Those who tell you the reasons you can't are the ones prompting your mind to find all the reasons you can,** and thus making it possible to create together solutions to any of the world's problems.

Third, compare your current Best Idea Ever to your previous Best Ideas Ever. Break them down side by side. If you are a truly gifted ADDer, you will find that you are breaking it down side by side by side by side by side . . . Today, I'm going through this exercise and realizing that I have so many irons in the fire, and if I don't get some things off my plate I'm never going to finish this book.

Use your E.O. We are not the best at realistic time frames and resource allocations. (Again, our gift and curse. Nothing truly great was considered realistic. The Wright Brothers? Crazy, and totally unrealistic!) When you make your comparisons, be honest with yourself about what should be priorities at this point in your life. If you have kids, you'll need to consider their ages, and how much time and influence you want to have in their lives. It's all too easy for an ADDer to go from one idea to the next, and before they know it, ten years went by and their kids never had a real mother or father. ADDers, by nature, take on more than they can handle. As forever optimists, and without an E.O.'s balancing perspective, they'll think to themselves, "Yeah, I can do that, too. I'll just be more productive." Don't fall into that trap. We are sprinters, and we need cool down time in our days. We will see Normals working a solid eight hour day and think, "If I buckle down and 'focus' I can do that too." Wrong. We work eighteen hours days, with random breaks mixed throughout to let our brains calm down. To others, and ourselves, it appears at times we aren't working efficiently at all. Not true. Our problem is we don't let our minds shut off even when we are away from work. In a 24-hour day, if we are not careful, our minds will work twenty-four hours.

Fourth, don't abandon a previous Best Idea Ever too soon. **Normals are always looking for a million dollar idea; ADDers are looking for the <u>next</u> million dollar idea.** We are never content with what we are doing; we want something new, because new is shiny. Stick with an idea for enough time to see it grow roots, and if possible stay on it until it starts to bear fruits. Only then can you leave it to your E.O.s to take care of without you. It's the early time in the creation of anything that there needs to be the most nurturing, and that incubator time needs the ADHD gifts. I'm saddened to see so many gifted ADDers abandon one great idea too soon to chase the next one, ultimately never succeeding at any of them.

For Normals, the challenge will always be coming up with a

great business idea, but when they do, they will stick with it. For ADDers, there are a million ways to make a million dollars. The challenge is sticking with it. Grab a good Equal-Opposite, and convince him or her to hang on for the ride. You can't ever promise success, but you can certainly promise them that it will be exciting! And I believe working together will be more rewarding than either of you could possibly dream of when doing it on your own.

When an "out there" business idea is brought up by an ADDer, you will clearly see the difference between a Normal and a good Equal-Opposite. The Normal will say things like, "That's a little unrealistic, isn't it?" or, "Let's keep our feet on the ground," or, "Aren't you being a little overly-optimistic?" The Equal-Opposites, however, will say things like, "Well then, let's look at all the possibilities," and, "Have you thought through the potential challenges, and what kind of changes we'll have to make to pursue this in a realistic way?" They are both similar in their comments, but a Normal is making statements of doubt based on their own bias. An E.O. questions to see where the ADDer is coming from, understanding the role is to support, uplift, and even channel the ADDer's talents and ideas in an effort to accomplish the goal, not diminish it. Ultimately, Equal-Opposites have realized that their life is full of excitement and success as a direct result of working for or with the ADDers of the world. Both E.O. and ADDers are enriched.

(UPDATE: Shortly after writing this chapter, Mr. Patey stepped down from his near full-time role in his largest company to free up mental horsepower and time for the new opportunity previously mentioned, and to finish this book without sacrificing time with his family. And there was much rejoicing.)

E.O. Comment:

For the E.O. this can be a very delicate challenge. Our initial reaction to another "opportunity" from an ADDer may be to immediately come up with all the reasons not to pursue it because it seems like a waste of time. Hear them out, though. Listen to everything before you jump to a conclusion.

Oftentimes, a great opportunity is hidden in what appears to be a distraction, and conversely, a perceived opportunity can often be just a distraction. This takes time to figure out, though, with discussion between both the ADDer and E.O.

The good news is that with practice, you learn how to read each other better and it becomes easier to sort the wheat from the chaff. Recognize that Normals often feel it is their job to put their ADDER's feet on the ground but sometimes you need to let them have their feet off the ground for a while to explore new ideas and options unhindered. A Normal that doesn't understand how to be a good E.O. will say "Let's be realistic." The good E.O. will say "Let's explore that."

—Dave

YOUR GENIUS, AMPLIFIED!

The ADHD Three Cs:

1. Consult

2. Compare

3. Cultivate, Couch, or Crush

(Yes, I know I'm cheating on the Three C's with Cultivate, Couch, or Crush, but bear with me and I'll explain.)

Like I've said, there are a million ways to make a million bucks, pick one . . . unless you have ADHD. In that case, pick three. Here's how:

You've got one to pay the bills, one you're most excited about, and one that percolates in the background. Then when a new idea comes percolatin',

Consult. your E.O. about your latest idea while it's fresh in your mind. Let the back-and-forth exploration happen naturally between the two of you.

Compare. your new idea or project with what's currently on your plate. How does it stack up? Would you give up one for the other? Will it detract from anything critical? E.O.'s are invaluable at this point. Realism and optimism finding common ground is the goal.

There is one of three possible places the idea will go from here. You will either Cultivate it, Couch it for later, or Crush it entirely.

Cultivate. This is a good idea that warrants more exploration. Be sure to only invest the time and resources you and your E.O. can agree on.

Couch. This is an intriguing idea, but it's not realistic to pursue it just yet. So you're going to let it rest for a bit. Remember, though, if you're going to couch it, YOU MUST COUCH IT. The ADHD mind has a hard time letting go of shiny objects, even if it's only temporary.

Crush. If you decide to scrap the idea, be prepared for the internal struggle. It helps if you ask yourself what negative things could occur if you fail to drop it.

In the event that you just can't crush it, then couch it for later. But the risk here is that you'll end up with so many things on the couch, you will never find a seat to relax in.

> "Even if you are on the right track, you'll get run over if you just sit there."
> — Will Rogers

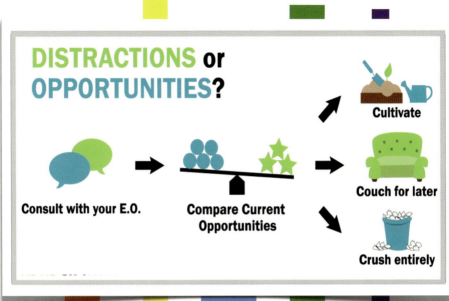

CHAPTER 9

DEATH OF A SUPERHERO

"The fastest way to destroy superheroes is to get them to believe they are not one."

~ Mark Patey

Imagine a high school track on a perfect spring day. In the center of the track is the football field, but today, instead of padded uniforms, it's filled with coaches, time keepers, and officials. It's the last track meet of the year: state finals. You've practiced diligently to get where you are today, and today you are the star, expected to win in every event. As the day progresses, you haven't disappointed; you're running smart and strong, exceeding expectations. It's now your last event, the 800-meter run. The 800 is grueling, but come hell or high water, you are going to win, even if it means you cross the finish line and collapse unconscious. As you line up on your mark, your heart pounds, adrenaline surges as the fans cheer from the stands. You can even make out the faint but distinctive sound of your loved ones calling your name in encouragement. The gun goes off, and you bolt from the line as if you were a bullet exiting the chamber of the starter's pistol. Your launch is so powerful, you're surprised the soles don't rip from the bottoms of your shoes. It's almost not fair; you're out front with superhero-like power, pushing you faster than you could ever have imagined. As you round the second turn of your first lap you notice the clock, and already your split time indicates that a new state—and maybe even national—record is going to be set today.

Encouraged by your time, you surge down the straight, pushing your pace beyond anything you've ever done. You're already a half lap ahead, an incredible feat by itself. The crowed cheers, but something else stands out most of all—an angry man yelling from the sideline. "Slow down! You're making the other kids feel bad!" *Why so bitter?* you wonder to yourself. But despite his discouragement you surge again. Not only are you going to win it, you're going to win it big!

As you round the last corner, your heart is pounding so hard you fear it's going to pop. Your lungs are on fire, and the intense pain from your legs is visible on your face, yet your speed continues to increase. With only 100 meters to go, the crowd is on its feet and the noise is deafening. Your vision blurs, the world around you darkens, but in that tunnel vision is the finish line. With the clock counting as if in slow motion, you realize you just might break a world record if you can push yourself one last time. *Head forward, chest forward, kick!*

you think to yourself. Everything you've got left is redirected and focused on your legs; you hear nothing, you feel nothing, you see only what you need to, and your pace quickens. The world seems silent, you're not aware of anything but the approaching finish line, and then you're there. The yellow ribbon pulls tight across your chest until it snaps, declaring you victorious. You've done it, you've broken every record, every expectation; truly, you are a superhero! Finally, you can stop running, but something's wrong. You're still sprinting, and the crowd's previous cheers of amazement are now silenced by their confusion. Your coach, teammates, and family are all screaming for you to stop, explaining that you're done. You're well aware you completed the race, but your legs aren't. It's like you're a huge snowball headed down the mountain—once it's up and going, it's pretty much impossible to stop. You plow through a crowd just past the finish line, sending those who were there to congratulate you toppling like bowling pins, yet you barely stumble. Panic begins to set in as you look back and notice that some of those you ran through are now on the ground injured and rolling in pain. Compounding the panic is your stark awareness that your heart can't handle what your legs continue to require of it. Your lungs are also past the failure point. You've heard of this kind of thing before. They call it LCHD, Leg Communication and Hyperactivity Disorder (note: not a real disorder.) Fear for your very life sets in as the realization comes that nothing you try and tell your legs is going to get them to stop.

E.O. Comment:

Each one of us has different talents and abilities. A great E.O. will recognize the gifts in an ADDer and help them channel those gifts for success. Look for those things that the ADDer is good at, and allow them to use those talents. There is a superhero in every one of us, and E.O.s need to be patient enough to see everyone for who they really are, and more importantly, who they can become. Often, many are blinded by the label of ADHD, making it impossible to be a great E.O.

-Dave

Only one thing to do, you think to yourself. *Force them to stop!* You aim for the wood fence paralleling the track on the far side and put your head down in preparation for the impact. Your family and friends are screaming for you to stop, but the rest of the crowd remains silent in shock at what's unfolding before their eyes.

Impact! The pain is almost too much to bear, yet you plow right through the fence without even slowing down. All that's changed is the blood now running down your cheek from a fresh gash at the edge of your hairline. "Stop!" you scream, while looking at your legs that continue to run without your permission. Turning back to the track where you can run without obstacles, you notice your coach is discussing options with a doctor and your family. They are all well aware that you can't continue running the way you have been for long; history has proven disastrous for those with LCHD.

The entire community is watching you self-destruct right before their eyes, when just moments ago you had such a bright future. You've lost control; even a normal life is out of the question for most with LCHD. The emotional pain begins to outweigh the physical. Your fear makes an unusual union with despair, and born out of that is Hopelessness. It's unlike anything you've experienced before. It creeps in, taking hold of everything with a numbing effect. All pain is gone from your body: your legs, your lungs, the cut on your forehead —you feel none of it. And even beyond that, you feel no concern at all for yourself, or even those loved ones around you. You know you should care, but somehow, you don't. With everyone you love watching you from nearby, somehow you have never felt so alone.

Meanwhile, as you struggle against the incredible strength of Hopelessness, a plan has been hatched on the sideline. A local law enforcement officer has retrieved a tranquilizer rifle from his trunk. Joining him on a golf cart is a doctor, your mother, and at the wheel is your track coach. You can't hear their conversation, but you know what's being said. The law officer is concerned that no other innocent citizens get hurt, the doctor sees no other options and is explaining to your mother the possible side affects of the drug carried in the dart, including possible permanent damage to the legs. Your coach is worried about what's going to happen to his star athlete (but what's the point of all that talent if it can't stay safely between the lines, or at least shut down and hold still when it's time?)

As they come up alongside you, the looks of compassion and pain are obvious from all on board. Their combined concern is for you and your best interests. The officer hands the tranquilizer rifle from the front seat back to the doctor.

"Here, Doc—you know what you need to do. I don't have a clear shot nor the authority to take it. This is a medical issue."

The doctor looks at the rifle and hands it off to your mother sitting to his left.

"Here, you're closest to him, and since he certainly has LCHD you may need to slow him down regularly in the future. You might as well get used to it."

Your mom looks down at the rifle with it's packaged drug, then raises it in your direction with tears running down her face. She shakes under the weight of the burden she now bears. "I'm sorry, son. I don't see any other way."

Your mind races, as if that super-powered strength in your legs just moved to your brain. In less time than it takes your mother to blink before pulling the trigger, you process everything that's happening. *Is this really the only way to get me to slow down? What if my heart and lungs could get stronger to handle what my legs can put out? What if this is really a gift, not a curse? I'm a track star! How can having such speed be so terrifying? What if I was given time to learn to leverage this strength to my advantage? What if I got a different coach? What is LCHD, anyway? Surely I'm not alone with this condition; surely others have learned to use it! Right?* Your self-talk slows as you see your mom pressing her finger up to the trigger. You quickly process your options. *I can choose to live with this new method of treatment, or choose to end it on my own terms.* **What is life if I can't live it being me?** You notice a concrete wall ahead and you bolt toward it without another thought, head down and sprinting as if it were the finish line. And it is: it's the finish line that can only be crossed when accompanied by Hopelessness. The world around you is in a panic. They want to save you from yourself, but in doing so, they may rob you of who you are—a runner.

Time slows. Only steps away from the wall, you close your eyes, drop your head and make your final surge as a superhero out of control. The distinct crack of a rifle shot echoes throughout the surrounding structures. You feel a pinch in your right thigh, and all goes dark as your body falls limp and slides in an explosion of dust, stopping just short of your intended finish.

When you wake, your family is around your hospital bed. They explain to you that you have a physical disorder that's found in a very small percentage of the population. You, in fact, do have LCHD, or Leg Communication and Hyperactivity Disorder. The doctor explains to you that they only have two options: cut your legs off, or medicate you to prevent your legs from ever working again. He explains that you can learn techniques to help you live without the use of your legs. In fact, there are all kinds of books, websites, support groups, public speakers, and experts that can help you live without the use of your legs. After all, your legs are dysfunctional; what if they misbehave again? As you listen, you realize that neither of the options includes the use of your legs, and certainly you will never be permitted to run again. You look down toward your feet and pull the blanket back to see your toes. You wiggle

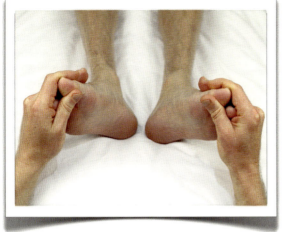 them slightly and smile in relief that they are still there. Noticing your smile, the doctor puts his hand on your leg and squeezes, then with a soft but stern voice looks you in the eyes and states, "They have a deficit and a disorder. You're going to have to learn to live without them, one way or another."

Imagine the pain you might experience if this really was you. A runner, told you could never use your legs again. What might this do to your psyche? What might happen to your self-worth? How appealing might drugs, alcohol, or other addictive distractions from reality become? And this, all this, is just your legs we are talking about. It's not like it's your brain! (I'm pausing for effect . . .) It's not like it's your *brain*!! When experts and loved ones tell us our brains have a disorder, it's devastating, and sometimes that devastation and hopelessness is irreversible. What if those with ADHD actually believe that they are "broken"? What kind of chance do they have? I intentionally use the word "broken," because that was the word used by all too many of the ADDicts I interviewed for this book. Is it any wonder that over half of people in drug rehab centers have ADHD? It wasn't the use of drugs that made them that way: studies show the diagnosis usually comes at a very early age, before the introduction to illegal drugs. I believe in many cases, it was the diagnosis of this pathology that broke their will and caused them to give up. The diagnosis was first, *then* the addictive behaviors came as part of a self-medicated "cure." I believe that ADHD is real in the sense that our brains function differently, but I refuse to accept it as a disorder. Certainly there are many challenges, but there are also many gifts that come from having a hyperactive brain.

Drugs do two things for people with ADHD: they react with the part of the brain that's in overdrive, bringing it back to a "normal," slower pace, and they also numb the emotional pain of being "broken" so that the diagnosed can continue to function despite, in their minds, being a second-class citizen. Interestingly, but not surprisingly, not one of the ADDers interviewed ever used the word "broken." As mentioned in another chapter, the ADDers interviewed for this book ALL rejected the experts' conclusion that ADHD was a disorder or pathology, and saw it only as a gift, with occasional "minor side effects."

> **DISTRACTION:**
> 2.7 million diagnosed with ADHD take medication (about 66%). -CDC (2007)

Our ADHD minds are like the legs that don't stop. They are sprinters, hyperactive sprinters, that are often capable of outrunning or outpacing many of those around us. What a gift! Remember the snowball? Once it gets up to speed, it's difficult to slow it down. What a curse! We lay in bed half the night because we can't get our minds to shut off. Ever wonder why there are so many ads for sleeping pills on ADHD web sites? If someone pulls the trigger and our mind starts the race, it's going to run whether we want it to or not. Not only that, it will run full steam ahead, regardless of what our teachers, co-workers or spouse want us to be doing at the time.

In the story above, the problem wasn't your speed. Sure, at times being exceptional might anger those who want to make sure everything is "fair," and that everyone feels good about themselves. You know the type—"everyone wins, everyone gets a trophy." They say they want people to achieve, but will then vilify anyone who does. Anyway, the problem wasn't your speed, you just didn't have a big enough track to run on. Same thing goes for the ADHD brain. On top of that, you need a place where your mind is free to sprint in whatever direction it wants from time to time. I'm not saying get out of school and self-educate or anything like that. I'm suggesting that you need to make sure you are in a learning environment that isn't so rigid as to limit your options on how YOU learn, or at what pace you learn. And with the ADHD gift, you learn at a very fast pace. Your grades aren't low because you're slow. Your grades tend to suffer because the class moves too slowly, and you get bored. Education should never

It's hard to use your powers when you're told they aren't "normal."

be your problem, the slow pace of education is. Compounding that problem is the fact that your genius mind likes to do its own thing. **Take a class that moves slowly plus a topic that is "boring" and you have a very "distracted" you.** Your mind will run off on its own in a full sprint, without your express written consent.

If an evil existed in the shadows of our world that wanted to destroy as many people as it could, it would find a way to crush the would-be leaders. It would destroy their self-worth, their very soul, by convincing them they were broken, and then just watch as they self-medicate and self-destruct, taking all of their potential with them. As I mentioned in "Deadly Blows," I don't believe for a second that any doctor, school teacher, or parent wakes up in the morning and thinks to him/herself "What can I do to destroy the self-worth of this individual today?" The challenge is that as long as people believe ADHD is a disorder, there is no way to tell someone they have it without crushing them. Word it any way you want, with all the sugar and sweetness you can muster:

"Oh Timmy, who I love more than life, you are such a great kid, that I love more than life, and also I love you so much, and I just wanted to tell you that you have a disability, a little disorder in you brain. I still love you so much, it's just that what we're trying to say is your brain is broken, or doesn't work like it is supposed to. But don't worry, little Timmy—there is only a 78% chance that it will stay broken for the rest of your life."

Of course you would use *much* better words. But seriously, it's like telling someone they have cancer in the brain, and there is no cure. It doesn't matter how you say it, the message is still the same: you are broken.

What we need is for the Normals of the world to graduate to true Equal-Opposites. People who truly believe in, recognize, and treat those with ADHD as equals, understanding that *different is not always a disorder.*

Imagine a world where a teacher, an Equal-Opposite, notices the ADHD traits in a student and smiles inside, knowing there is a truly gifted child in their class. Then the teacher calls the parents in and says: "I've been watching your child, I think he has a gift. It's called the ADHD gift. His mind most likely moves faster than other kids' minds, and is capable of thinking in multiple directions at once. This is very exciting, but it can also be a challenge at times. Studies are now showing that kids with this gift can get bored and distracted easily because of their high intelligence. I believe your son is an Einstein. In fact, Einstein, Abraham Lincoln, Bill Gates, Thomas Edison, and countless others of a similar yoke were blessed and challenged with this very same gift. I suggest we work with him, push him a little, maybe even test him to see if he does in fact have the gift."

How might the parents feel with this message, instead of what they are hearing today:

"We fear your son has Attention Deficit Hyperactivity Disorder, and we suggest you consider medicating him and putting him in resource classes."

Ouch.

Note: Why did I call this chapter "Death of a Superhero"? Simple: because it sounded so much cooler than "Runner Gets Bad News." That, and there is a slight possibility that it was an analogy exploring the emotional death of an exceptional individual.

Too heavy? Don't worry. The next chapter, "I'm Bored," has a happy ending. Read on, dear reader.

So, young ADDer, how much potential do **you** have?

Exactly.

Death of a Superhero
TAKEAWAYS:

✓ Recognize that sometimes medication is a necessary crutch—try to make it a temporary one.

✓ Some meds may limit our brains' ability to "run" at full speed.

✓ Your ADHD brain is designed to go fast, so let it!

YOUR GENIUS, AMPLIFIED!

The ADHD Hero Three

1. Accept
2. Recognize
3. Develop

Accept that you might be a superhero in embryo. Power unrealized is useless, and power uncontrolled can be dangerous. So understand that despite the challenges that come along for the ride, you've been given some pretty amazing abilities. Haven't found them yet? No worries–they're there. And accepting that you've got incredible potential is the first step towards unlocking them.

Recognize that mediocrity will always be threatened by exceptionalism. And also realize that doesn't mean you need to hide who you are so that someone else might not feel like less. One of my favorite quotes says:

"As we let our own light shine,

we unconsciously give others permission to do the same."

-Marianne Williamson

In my experience, those who see excellence as a threat are those who are afraid to strive for it. Fine, let them rage and stomp their feet. In the meantime, you'll be out there actually doing something. Do not let anyone tell you that by being you, you're doing it wrong. Do not let anyone tell you that you're anything less than who you are.

Develop your ADHD mind by letting it run on larger tracks with the freedom of flexibility. Are there times when you need to rein it in a bit? Absolutely. Certain settings just aren't suitable for the ADHD energy (lectures, board meetings, defusing explosives, etc.) But once you've accepted your potential and recognized that it's nothing to be ashamed of, you've got to nurture the gifts. Giving your brain the regular workouts that it needs. Creating, problem-solving, tinkering, etc. will train it to perform at its best.

> **"It is surmounting difficulties that makes heroes."**
>
> -Louis Pasteur

CHAPTER 10

I'M BORED

"Mom, mom, mummy, mother, mom . . . I'm bored." I want to laugh and cry at the same time as I remember the look on my mom's face as my brother Mike and I made this comment repeatedly, almost hourly, throughout our childhood. Summers must have been outright torture for her. We were hyperactive twins longing for something to do, but never seeming to find enough. Back then, we didn't have the choices on TV like we do now. At night there was *The Dukes of Hazard*, but that was only for an hour, and we didn't care about the news. For daytime TV there was *Sesame Street*, but that was for babies, not young men like me and Mike. We were far too cool to admit to watching that. . . . There was no internet, and videos games were something only our "rich" friends had. To my mother, the only thing that was worse than the statement "I'm bored" was the inevitable follow-up question, "What can I do?"

> **E.O. Comment:**
>
> The E.O. needs to realize that ADDers need something to work on to occupy their minds, oftentimes even during other activities. Provide constructive opportunities, even though it may be challenging. As Mark and I travel for business, there is little downtime at all. Even when we're flying in our plane and he's managing all of the instruments, radio, ATIS, ATC, etc., I bring my iPad, brainstorm business ideas, work on this book or others yet to come, sign contracts, discuss new inventions, etc.
>
> As an E.O., always have something positive to write about, watch, or discuss. Your ADDer will always need something to do, so it might as well be constructive and uplifting.
>
> —Dave

If you're the parent of an ADHD child, you can relate. (Distraction: please note I did not refer to the child as an ADDer, but rather as someone with ADHD. This is intentional. There is a distinct difference. Remember, an ADDer is someone leveraging their ADHD gift to their advantage and is contributing, or "adding," to the world around them. Children usually haven't yet learned these critical leveraging skills.) Two of my four children have ADHD, and this has been eye-opening. Watching my wife interact with our ADHD sons has been educational, as she repeatedly attempts to give them household chores or some sort of meaningless assignment when they're bored. She'd try anything if it worked just long enough for her to take care of her own busy day. This attempt to buy herself time, of course, never works and never will with ADHD kids, nor ADHD adults for that matter. Why, you might ask? It's important to understand what is really being said when a child with ADHD says "I'm bored."

First of all, it's imperative to remember that boredom is a sign of high intelligence. A cow is completely content to stand in a field and watch the grass grow, however Albert Einstein would pull his hair out and go crazy. (Please cow lovers, no hate mail. It's simply a comparative analogy.)

The higher the intelligence, the greater the need for stimulation to the brain to prevent boredom. When someone with ADHD says, "I'm bored," what they are essentially saying is, "My mind has nothing to do." Any attempt to give them a strictly physical task will do nothing to "cure" the boredom. It's as pointless as trying to cure a backache by pulling a tooth (plus, now there are *two* things bothering you.) You must deal with the boredom first: engage their hyperactive genius brains with something productive. A few important tips to keep in mind when choosing things that will cure the boredom:

"When all think alike, then no one is thinking."
-Walter Lippman

- ☑ The ADHD brain moves fast.

- ☑ The ADHD brain loves to solve problems.

- ☑ The ADHD brain likes to go in its own directions.

- ☑ The ADHD brain moves out from an idea, or trigger, in all directions at once; it doesn't follow a linear path, so give it some flexibility and freedom to turn on a dime.

- ☑ The ADHD brain is competitive.

- ☑ The ADHD brain enjoys physical activity if it's engaging the brain. (Why do you think we can't hold still? Also explains why so many successful athletes have ADHD—Michael Jordan for example.)

- ☑ The ADHD brain feeds on instant gratification and loves stimulus any way it can find it.

- ☑ DO NOT stick its nose in a corner, figuratively or physically. It will self-destruct.

Secondly, when an ADHD individual says "I'm bored," it is critical (yes, I said CRITICAL, as in life and death) to remember that boredom is a kind of depression. Based on your increasing knowledge of the ADHD mind, you can see how easy it can be for anyone with high intelligence to fall into a deep depression. In fact, people with ADHD are 2.7 times more likely to suffer from depression than Normals. If you find yourself on the boredom truck, watch out. Depression is the trailer attached to that truck, and it's carrying a cargo full of addictive behaviors as an alternative distraction to the pain of boredom.

Wouldn't it be better to keep that brain active and happily productive? One more point on boredom: Alcoholics Anonymous and other effective treatment programs use a common acronym for what triggers addictive behaviors—BLAST. It stands for Bored, Lonely, Anxious, Stressed, Tired. These are the major pitfalls for anyone dealing with addiction, but particularly dangerous for those with ADHD is the first item on the list, because we are so much more easily bored than Normals.

A word of caution: we are often tempted to allow our bored children to play video games. Games are such cheap baby sitters. And while perhaps not a big deal for Normals, to the ADHD brain, video games are like crack cocaine! The games are fast; require problem solving; can go in different directions all at once; are competitive; provide instant gratification with points, discoveries, powers, abilities, etc.; and they engage you physically through the controls, emotionally through story lines, visually with stunning graphics, and audibly with fantastic stereo effects. I discovered at the age of twenty-eight that I was a gaming addict. It took only one game. I stayed up for days without sleep and skipped work. I'm lucky I owned my own company as it could have cost me my job, otherwise. When I finished the game, I was finally able to walk away from it, and I haven't touched a game since, not even for one second to play with my kids. Even more concerning is that many games nowadays don't have an end, and when an ADHD brain really triggers on something, it will push and push for a finish, especially if the

journey is fun.

My little brother, Aaron, is as ADHD as they come. In school he was always the class clown, consistently finding ways to entertain himself and those around him. This resulted in regular visits to the principal's office, yet somehow his people-pleasing talents kept him from getting into any real trouble. When asked why he couldn't sit still in class and pay attention, his reply was always the same: "I'm bored." Eventually, he got so bored of school that he'd only show up to hang out with his friends and decide where they would go to skip class that day. As an obvious result his grades suffered, and his self-worth, which is directly connected to personal responsibility, suffered as well. So here's a high school kid diagnosed with a disorder and burdened with the label and self-doubt that goes with it. On top of that, Aaron is bored—a symptom of depression, and also the first trigger on the list of addictive pitfalls. Any guesses as to the rest of the story? Anyone? Anyone? "Bueller . . . ? Bueller . . . ?" (Shameless 80s movie reference.)

Yes! *Ding ding ding!* You guessed right: Aaron started doing drugs. Pain pills, to be specific.

Aaron dropped out of high school with a laundry list of failing grades preceding the final goodbye. After all, what's the point of torturing yourself in a boring class if you aren't ever going to be "smart" anyway? Aaron came to work for Mike and me, doing general labor on construction sites. He was worthless at digging holes, hauling lumber, almost anything you would put an "uneducated" man to work doing—he was always distracted. You couldn't keep him on task for anything. Mike and I talked on many occasions about letting him go, but that's a tough thing to do when you're trying to get a loved one on their feet and off of drugs. Plus, where could a high-school-drop-out, pill-popping ADHD kid possibly go? Besides jail, I mean. So we kept him on, like a charity case.

We got a concerned call one day from a crew foreman out on a job. He had spent hours on a problem set of stairs, but he couldn't figure out how to set a very complex riser on a turn to make sure the stairs landed exactly where they needed to go. The call was to get us to come out and see if we could get the math to work. When we got there, though, Aaron was just finishing up explaining to the foreman where his geometry was off and why the numbers weren't working. I looked at Mike after examining the problem and solution and commented, "I don't think I could have figured out that one." Mike agreed. From that point on, we pushed Aaron to complex projects, and he shined. Soon he was not only running the fastest crew in the company, but he could handle multiple jobs at the same time without missing a thing. The more complex the problem, the less he got "distracted." He thrived on creative problem solving; I would even go so far as to say he lived for it, like it was an addictive game.

    Aaron decided to take the GED test. When asked why, his response was simple. "I just want to prove to *myself* that I'm not as stupid as people thought I was." He passed without studying. His mind had been absorbing everything in school like a sponge; it was his teachers that had always believed the ridiculous notion that eye contact somehow equaled listening. They thought if he wasn't looking at them, then certainly he wasn't hearing them (as if eyes and ears are somehow codependent). I've since noticed that if you watch an ADDer's eyes when they are really processing something on a deep level, their eyes are darting around while looking downward, almost as if they're searching a card file index in fast forward. The looking away for an ADDer is often because they *are* listening and truly processing on multiple levels, not the other way around. It only *looks* like a distracted individual. Oh, teachers, parents . . . please reread that.

    Aaron became the most valuable employee we ever had, but like all good things it had to come to an end. Aaron's ADHD gift really blossomed as he learned to leverage it to his advantage.   He stopped self-medicating, and he grew to realize he didn't need to be anyone's employee. He left us to chase his own business ideas and found great success. And not just once—Aaron built two successful businesses within the next few years.

    Distraction: I don't believe it's entirely possible for an ADDer to truly retire. We are, after all, serial entrepreneurs, addicted to the creative and creating process.

Aaron was just another kid with ADHD, who became another statistic in a long list of people with ADHD who become ADDicts. He could easily have stayed there, digging holes and doing a lousy job at it, but instead he became an ADDer. ADDicts and Millionaires—so close to the same thing it's scary.

When kids aren't challenged, they'll figure something out on their own.

YOUR GENIUS, AMPLIFIED!

"Excuse me world. May I have permission to feel good about myself?" Sounds like a ridiculous question, doesn't it? Almost as if it were a child asking to leave a class to use the bathroom. Yet this is how many operate in life without even knowing it. My brother felt that somehow, despite all his achievements, he needed to go back and take a high school exam to get his GED. Why? Certainly, getting a GED is a good thing, but that's not what I'm getting at. Like so many of us, he had adopted a viral notion, a disease of thought, that unless we have the papers to prove we are of value (or educated), we aren't.

I fear for the future of any individual, or nation, that propagates the notion that somehow academic credentials carry more value than actual accomplishments. Formal education is a key component of success and can be invaluable, but as soon as success itself is deemed unworthy evidence of education (albeit not formal), we've failed as a society.   Education comes in many forms: a university, an apprenticeship, a self-driven consumption of knowledge through reading and study, or experience.

The sad truth is this: our education system hasn't fully figured out how to teach those with ADHD. As a result, many brilliant minds drop out and give up on formal education, and if that's not bad enough, they drop out with the belief that they can't learn, and subsequently give up on themselves. It's up to us to change that.

We learn differently, and that's okay. In fact, I do hereby irrevocably decree that you have permission to feel good about yourself, and you may celebrate all your accomplishments as the successes in education that they are. Continue to learn, devouring all that interests you, and you will find success, a sense of accomplishment, and most importantly, a sense of value that comes from within.

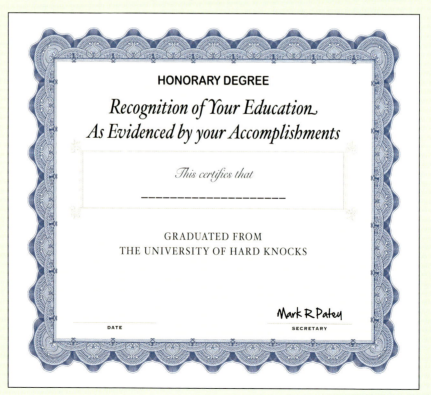

I'm Bored! TAKEAWAYS:

- ✓ Bored? Hello, Genius! (Boredom is an indicator of intelligence.)
- ✓ The ADHD brain moves quickly.
- ✓ It LOVES to solve problems.
- ✓ It likes to go in its own direction, and often in multiple directions.
- ✓ It needs flexibility.
- ✓ It's competitive.
- ✓ It enjoys physical activity if it's mentally engaging.
- ✓ It loves stimulus any way it can find it.
- ✓ Don't stick its nose in the corner, or it will self-destruct.

Only in America can a self-educated farm boy become the 16th president.

"What he has in the way of education, he has picked up." Abraham Lincoln (ADHD) wrote this statement in a 3,000 word autobiography during his presidential campaign. At the age of ten, he attended school in Indiana, but school terms were far shorter than they are today. Abraham might attend school for one to three months in the winter and then he would be expected to help out on the family farm. Trying to learn anything in just a few months each year was hard enough, but to make things worse country teachers were not always well educated. Lincoln remembered, "no qualification was ever required of a teacher, beyond readin', writin', and cipherin'." The educational system did not help most children become interested in learning. Abraham, however, was not like most children.

-history4kids.info

CHAPTER 11

THE BEST QUESTION IN THE WORLD

*"We learn more by looking for the answer
to a question and not finding it than we
do from learning the answer itself."*

~ Lloyd Alexander

There is one question that tops all other questions. It is, in fact, the most powerful question in the world. (By the way, this is best read in a deep voice with intense music, like the guy that announces upcoming movies during the previews: "IN A WORLD . . .") This question can be asked of anything, of anyone, at any time, and at any place. The question itself has led to nearly every discovery on planet Earth, and probably on any other worlds that might be out there. It was the precursor

> **DiSTRACTiON (kind of): Where did the Question Mark come from?**
> The story goes that the question mark actually originated from the Latin word "qvaestio," meaning "question." This word was reportedly abbreviated in the Middle Ages by scholars as just "qo." Eventually, a capital "Q" was written over the "o," and it formed one letter. Then, it morphed into the modern question mark we know today. There's not much actual evidence to support this claim, but it's still a fun explanation!
>
> quaestio   q———o   qo   ? ? ? ?

to every invention. The catalyst to every abstract thought. It separates man from animals even more than the opposable thumb. The question itself is so magnificent, it has stumped the minds of even the most brilliant among us throughout the ages. It is, in fact, the question that led to every discovery in all of the sciences. In physical science, including chemistry, mathematics, and physics. The social sciences, including psychology, cognitive sciences, and sustainability. Biological sciences, including biochemistry, microbiology, cell studies, anthropology, computational ecology, genetics, and neurophysiology, just to name a few. They all came from one simple question: WHY? Yes, WHY? (followed closely by its identical twin brother, HOW?) has delivered to humankind almost every great breakthrough and invention we now enjoy. And the continuation of this constant questioning will lead us to countless more discoveries, even the inevitable and ongoing discovery that what we now know to be true will no longer be true in the future, and that a greater and more perfect truth exists. What is being human if not to progress? And progress is impossible without constantly questioning.

The ADHD mind is definitely different than normal minds. One way it differs is it's constantly asking those two powerful questions: "Why?" and "How?" And the answers are like a drug that the ADHD mind can't get enough of. It *needs* to understand how everything works, it *must* fit things together, and it *has to* understand the relationship between all things. It's also often incapable of just accepting an answer without an explanation. Yet those best positioned to encourage this gift of constant questioning are often the ones who unwittingly discourage it, and even turn it off at early ages.

Junior high school, 1985. It was the first week of school, and I was in a welding class that I had been looking forward to for years. When the teacher started talking about the welders we would be using, I asked a simple question,

"How does a welder work?"

His answer was short.

"It uses electricity to heat the metal enough to melt it and create a bond between two or more pieces of metal."

A normal mind, or child, might be satisfied with that answer. I followed up.

"How does it get it that hot?"

This was just an ADHD mind doing what it does, looking for an understanding of *why* something works the way it does. To my teacher, it was a deviation from his curriculum, but he answered, somewhat abruptly.

"It uses upwards of 500 amps of electricity to get it that hot."

Again, my ADHD mind wanted more, so I kept asking.

"How can it put 500 amps into the weld when the welder itself is only plugged into a 220 volt outlet on a 50 amp circuit?"

Now he was visibly bothered. Maybe it was because he thought I was being a smart aleck, or maybe because I didn't raise my hand. It could have been because I pressed him, a teacher, to the edge of his knowledge in front of everyone, thus possibly damaging his ego. I'll never know for sure, but his reply sent a clear signal.

"That will be enough questions."

Message received loud and clear—I wasn't to push for knowledge beyond what he had planned to offer me. I wasn't to ask questions. Just sit still, shut up, and listen. But what about learning? He was right about the high amps coming from the welder, but he didn't know how it converted it from 220 volts. Maybe he didn't care how it worked, just that it worked. One thing I can guarantee about that teacher . . . he will never invent a better welder, a more efficient welder, or a different way of welding. He is done with the *why* in his life, and is content with the *it just is* rule of life and everything in it. I think that's tragic. And even more tragic than that, his students will learn to listen but they will NEVER learn to learn. They will never learn to think on their

own and to question everything, only to accept what's being taught. How sad, and how truly terrifying. What if what's being taught in our schools is wrong? History has proven that most things over time are not what we thought they were originally.

As a child, I took everything apart. Tape decks, VCRs, broken engines, electric can openers, literally anything I could get my hands on. My twin brother, Mike, and I would head to a small dump within biking distance of our house nearly every weekend to scavenge for stuff to make something with. We had no idea what we would make, or what we were looking for, but inevitably we would see something that would make our minds trigger. Ideas blossomed, and soon our wagon was once again on its way home tied behind one of our bikes, full of our ideas and dreams. On more than one occasion, an older neighborhood kid stopped us and teasingly asked, "What are you guys going to build with that trash today? A bigger pile of trash?" Thankfully, our self-worth was strong enough to ignore it, and we would keep riding without engaging the emotional bully. Once home, my mom would roll her eyes knowing the mess was just getting started, and my dad resigned himself to the fact that once again it was guaranteed he wouldn't be able to find his tools next time he needed them. But one thing they never did—they never discouraged us. In fact, on multiple occasions, dad brought something home that someone was going to throw away, and would unveil it like it was a gift from Santa. "Mike! Mark!" he would yell with enthusiasm, "I've got something I bet you're going to love." We would come running and he'd show us whatever he had found. Excitedly, we would head to the garage with the junk to start the disassemble-and-creatively-reassemble process. Our reputation for "frankenstein-ing" everything was legendary. The electric can-opener became a winch to pull things from one

cardboard fort to another, the TV became a strange light in our furniture/blanket tents, an old drill powered us around on a converted skateboard as far as our extension cords could reach. I remember visiting the neighbors for a Christmas get-together where I saw for the first time a large windup clock. I picked it up with a great deal of curiosity, and while examining it closely, said out loud, "I've never seen inside a clock before." The homeowner, Perry, literally ran to my side, snatched the clock from my hands, and with a concerned voice said to my father, "Ken Patey, you keep your kids away from my clock." My dad just laughed. Shortly after, Perry brought us a broken clock and said, "Here, take this one apart." Oh, how I loved discovery, and still do. We must never detract from that creative curiosity in an ADHD child or adult: it's what a hyperactive mind needs to survive, and thrive.

Mike and I have a particular fascination with all things mechanical. However, that desire in the ADHD brain to understand how things work is not limited to taking things apart and putting them back together. ADDers find that creative curiosity most powerful or interesting when trying to understand how relationships work, or how business works, or how the universe works. It could be anything; the universal needs of the active ADHD brain are to learn, to understand, to make connections, to fix the broken, to create something new, or to improve something that already exists. What a powerful gift. And as long as that desire for understanding isn't shut down by the doubters or quenched by those unwilling to answer questions, or those unwilling to question everything, even their own knowledge, the ADDers of the world will continue to create. This need for an ADHD brain to connect dots and see a much larger picture is why the ADDers do so well in business, and it's also why they tend to enjoy games that require skill, strategy, and problem solving over games left to chance.

If you rob someone with ADHD of their naturally occurring curiosity, you will find they will self-medicate to entertain or numb that part of their inquisitive genius brain. Some say curiosity killed the cat. I say not allowing curiosity to be satisfied with facts is what created the ADDicts. Curiosity hasn't killed me. Sure, it has electrocuted me on many occasions, but it hasn't killed me. In fact, the opposite has been true: I believe curiosity is the mother of invention more than necessity. When the rest of us need something, we will invent to fill that need. ADDers, on the other hand, create even when there is no perceived need. Who needed commercially available lightbulbs when we had candles and lanterns? Thomas Edison had ADHD, and was he ever curious. Who needed another way to communicate? Talking face to face seemed to work just fine, and if someone lived away, you wrote them a letter. Alexander Graham Bell had ADHD, and he figured out how to communicate over a wire. Who needs another spaceship for travel to outer space, when we have the space shuttles? Burt Rutan and Richard Branson, both ADHD, thought is was too expensive to do it the way NASA does it and created SpaceShipOne in response.

It's one thing to see a need and fill that need. It's an entirely different thing to see needs that nobody else is seeing and create toward that end, thus creating the need itself. A common theme among the self-made millionaires/ADDers interviewed for this book was that their businesses were, for the most part, created out of something nobody else had considered beforehand. It wasn't until after they created a need that others began to pursue the same business plans or products. Am I suggesting that only ADDers can invent and create? Certainly not. However, historically they have done a very good job at it, and we are finding that statistically they are more likely than the "normal" people to create outside the proverbial box. Heck, we are so outside the box we couldn't find the box or tell you what it looks like. Out of fifty self-made millionaires studied for this book, over half had ADHD, yet it's estimated that only 7% of the US population has ADHD. That puts an ADDer at three times the likelihood to create wealth and jobs than the rest of the population. Sorry to poke the experts in the eye on this one, but maybe, just maybe, we aren't as broken as the "experts" have been telling us. We are just different. And **different is not a disorder**. Moreover, maybe everyone has a little crazy ADHD in them, and I believe it's about time we work to wake it up. A quick search on the internet for "creativity in children destroyed" will give you several studies showing that creativity in children is largely destroyed by the second grade! What?! Here's a sad hypothesis: maybe the system just "fixed" the ADHD we all were blessed with as children. Whatever caused it, it makes me sad. It's like watching a puppy get hit by a car, or a bully stepping on a kid's sand castle. It's just not right.

My dad created a seminar series called "Creating a Climate For Growth," in which he wrote the following:

A CHILD'S WINDOW ON THE WORLD

Think back to the last time you looked at the world through the eyes of a child. Picture, if you will, the following two scenarios: The setting for both is identical. The weather is warm, the blue sky is adorned here and there with white puffy clouds, the grass and the flowers and trees in the park are picture-perfect.

The first scenario includes a mother who obviously wants to walk faster along the pathway through the park than her almost-two-year-old toddler. He continually slows, reaches for things on the pathway or the edge of the grass, making attempts to leave the path, and stopping repeatedly, constantly "distracted." The more he delays his mother, the more annoyed and frustrated she becomes. What we see finally is the mother holding either the child's hand or wrist firmly and with some determination pulling the child down the pathway. The toddler emits whimpering cries and stumbles repeatedly as his little legs struggle to keep up with the exasperated mother who is determinedly maintaining her preferred pace.

For the second scenario, picture the same mother and toddler on the same pathway. You can hardly say they are walking. Instead, it is, at best, a sauntering. Perhaps more accurately said, it is more a stop and go, with emphasis on the stop! Given the freedom to pause at will, the toddler will be exploring EVERYTHING he sees. He squats down, picks up something he has seen on the ground and examines it intently. If the mother is sensitive to a child's learning processes, her toddler will be sharing with her what he is

discovering. She will frequently place herself at his level, even sitting for periods of time next to him on the pathway or on the grass. What she will be seeing in his eyes and face is his excitement and awe and wonder at this world within his grasp. Does she need to examine an ant, or a twig, or some pebble? Hardly! "Been there and done that!" What she will be witnessing, if she is alert, is the beginning of the expansion of the child's world and his understanding of it. And given this kind of sensitivity on the part of OTHER adults, his love for learning and his capacity for understanding will continually expand

and increase! (Note: Now go back and replace "mother" with "teacher" or "employer" in both scenarios. You get the picture.)

Yes, those with ADHD leave the trail a lot. We bounce around from one shiny object to the next, exploring different directions all at the same time, it seems. We are constantly distracted with the world around us . . . what a gift! Question everything! And never stop asking yourself, and others, that beautifully simple and powerful question:

E.O Comment:

It can be easy to become frustrated with the seemingly endless curiosity of an ADDer especially now that there's so much information at our fingertips from the internet (Wikipedia, YouTube, etc.) They have an endless supply of answers to questions through our current mediums of learning, which can make it tough for them to concentrate on the task at hand.

As an E.O., understand that this natural inquisitiveness empowers the ADDer to find solutions to problems that a Normal may not have the energy to pursue. I can't even begin to count the times when I personally didn't see a solution to a problem even after hours of brainstorming, but when I discussed it with Mark, within minutes we had it figured out. The ADDer ability to chase the "Why?" and the "How?" down to the core has provided us with airplanes, electricity, wifi, computers, etc. . . . An ADDer and an E.O, both with a core belief that there is a solution to every problem, will usually find it.

-Dave

YOUR GENIUS, AMPLIFIED!

Curiosity didn't kill the cat, but discouraging curiosity killed the ADHD gift, and replaced it with the ADHD curse.

Not only do we need to put an end to all the discouragement those with ADHD get when they are "distracted," but we need to come fully around and encourage those "distractions" and turn them into learning experiences.

Push pause in your busy life schedule to allow the ADHD brain to discover and learn about what has "distracted" it. Added benefit; Once it has learned all it can about the subject, it will no longer be distracted by it.

Provide an environment where you can explore, experiment, and discover. This is hard-core brain exercise for those with ADHD. During these workouts, you will learn automatically how to connect the dots between seemingly unrelated items, and program, or even internally wire, the brain for success in problem-solving for the future.

> "Millions saw the apple fall, but Newton was the one who asked why."
> -Bernard Baruch

The Best Question in the World

TAKEAWAYS:

Ask! Ask!

✓ Questions can be frustrating, but must be encouraged!

✓ ADHDers are curious, curiosity leads to knowledge, which leads to experience, which leads to wisdom.

✓ Engage the ADHD brain. Put it into gear instead of shutting it down.

Ask! Ask! Ask! Ask! Ask! Ask! Ask! Ask!

Curiosity has lead to some pretty great things.

(Even if they did look kind of funny at first . . .)

CHAPTER 12

HEALTHY A<u>DD</u>ICTIONS

(Because the suggestions in this chapter are uniquely designed for the ADD mind!)

The idea of a healthy addiction is so contrary to common logic that to even hear someone say "Healthy addictions" seems to shock the senses. It's a perfect oxymoron, like saying "Military Intelligence," "Government Efficiencies," or my favorite, the "Affordable Tax." But this subject must be addressed, at least in part, if we are to help those with ADHD find success.

addiction |əˈdikSHən|:
noun
the fact or condition of being addicted to a particular substance, thing, or activity: *he committed the theft to finance his drug* addiction | *an* addiction *to gambling.*

One of the questions asked of every person interviewed for this book was, "Do you have any addictive behaviors?" It may be of no surprise to anyone

that 100% of the ADDicts interviewed for this book replied affirmatively; they admitted to addictive behaviors, and in most cases were not shy about revealing their illegal drug preferences. However, they were understandably more reserved about discussing sexual ADDictions, as such is not openly talked about in our culture despite its prevalence. Not surprisingly, video gaming ADDictions were very common, as games these days are so perfectly built for the ADHD brain. That's not to say programmers are in any way going after the ADHD crowd intentionally. And please programmers, don't write me any hate mail. Your games are just so "shiny." (Again, I'm a recovering gaming ADDict—not one game since 1996.)

When asked of the Millionaires, "Do you have any addictive behaviors?" The ADDers' responses were quite surprising, even shocking! 100% of the ADDers replied affirmatively! Yes, all of ADDers, just like the ADDicts, had addictive behaviors. *Wait, what?! Mark, are you saying all the millionaires were addicts as well?* No, not all the millionaires. What I'm saying is, of all the millionaires, those that with ADHD said they had addictive behaviors. Reminder: over half of the millionaires interviewed for this book had ADHD and are referred to as ADDers. Also over half of the drug addicts interviewed had ADHD and are referred to as ADDicts. So, in short, all those with ADHD studied for this book were "victims" of addictive behaviors. OMG . . . They all self-medicated—the difference was only the method of self-medication.

<u>Addict begins with ADD.</u> You can't take the ADD out of ADDict, and you can't take the addict out of those with ADD/ADHD. I know this is painful to hear, and I'm sure there are exceptions out there somewhere, but I'll bet dollars-to-dimes those exceptions are few and far between. We, as a whole, have very addictive personalities. (Keep reading: the pain and denial you might be

experiencing now will be traded for hope and enthusiasm in a bit. Just give me a little leeway before you close your mind or make assumptions)

Much has been said on the subject of ADHD and addictive behaviors, but always only in the negative. This drives me nuts. There are also many positives to addictive personalities, if correctly understood and leveraged to one's advantage. If you study the addictive behaviors and traits of those with ADHD coupled with the misconceived idea that ADHD is wholly a deficit and a disorder, the only thing you will find in your studies are the negative traits and evidences supporting that hypothesis. All studies will forever be slanted in favor of the original premise of the argument. My contention is that the original premise, that ADHD is a disorder, is false.

Different is not a disorder.

Before writing this book, I argued until I was blue in the face that people with ADHD are no more subject to addiction than anyone else. I didn't want to believe it, despite all the evidence. To accept it was to accept a seemingly unchangeable fault, or to accept that somehow I was broken and could not be fixed. I was in denial even about my own addictive behaviors. But now after conducting my own study I concede that, on this point, the experts are right. All of my ADHD interviews confirmed that we are, in fact, addicts by nature. HOWEVER, not all addictions have to be unhealthy!

Having an addictive personality certainly can be a curse. But, by studying successful ADDers, we learn it can be a gift as well—if properly understood and put into the proper perspective. Many "normal" addicts are taught to find a hobby to replace their addictive behavior. This is a good technique and can be effective for Normals as long as they enjoy the hobby. For an ADDer or ADDict, though, there are a few additional components that are critical:

Recognize and **accept** that you have an addictive personality. Then seek diligently to find healthy addictions, lest the unhealthy ones slip in and destroy you. Here are three tips to finding healthy addictions:

1st **Recognize** and **accept** that we are multitasking machines with hyperactive brains that must do more than one thing at a time (otherwise we get bored).

We bore easily!

2nd Remember, boredom is the first trigger that leads to unhealthy addictive behaviors. (BLAST = Bored, Lonely, Anxious, Stressed, Tired). Our "hobby" can't just be any hobby we enjoy—it must also engage the brain on at least two levels (more would be better). For example, putting together a model in a quiet room WILL NOT WORK. Doing a crossword puzzle while listening to your favorite talk radio program just might, assuming you enjoy crossword puzzles.

3rd Healthy addictions for an ADDict or ADDer **MUST HAVE A DISTINCT START AND FINISH**. When the ADHD brain "spools up" or fully engages in a project or activity of interest it wants to stay there. We will work all night long to finish a project even if it means no sleep for the important work day tomorrow. We will ignore the otherwise obvious negative outcomes because we've become hyper-focused on the task at hand. I believe this is for two reasons: 1) We thrive when we get our brains really engaged. We feed on it like a drug; there is an adrenaline-like effect, and that's a drug we enjoy. 2) We know subconsciously that when we disengage from the project we may never get back to it, because there will always be something else trying to engage us.

★ **RECOGNIZE** THE ADDICTIVE NATURE OF THE ADHD BRAIN AND PICK A HEALTHY ADDICTION.
★ HEALTHY ADDICTIONS MUST **ENGAGE** THE ADHD BRAIN ON AT LEAST TWO LEVELS.
★ HEALTHY ADDICTIONS MUST HAVE A DEFINED **START AND FINISH**.

This is not to say that if you're ADHD you *have* to have an addictive behavior. It's not a requirement to get into the club, or anything. However, it may be a healthy consideration. When you have a brain that tends to go in multiple directions, all at the same time, a healthy addiction can become grounding, and add the very consistency that your mind needs. So is that what the ADDers have figured out? For the most part, yes, but they still need to make sure they focus on the components above. For reference, the following examples are some common addictions found in the ADDers I interviewed:

> **DiSTRACTiON:** "Americans who report they are 'very concerned' about stress exercise less. Roughly a third (36%) said that they didn't exercise in the last week. **Exercise remains one of the healthiest ways to deal with stress.**"
> -Bill Erb, LPC, NBCC

"I'm addicted to my work." *Kristen L.*

This was a very common response, and though it can be a gift, and explains in part the incredible levels of success in many of the ADDers, this can also be a curse. It certainly engages the brain on multiple levels, particularly if you are in a high-level position or are the owner. You have to track multiple variables at all times, predict potential outcomes, problem solve continually, etc. Here's the challenge, though: if you're the owner, you might not ever go home. Family suffers, health suffers, and there is nothing resembling a balanced life because there is no defined "FINISH." The dynamics can change if you are not an owner and work a similar role, but have a defined start and end time to the day. People with ADHD are often great salespeople, and their time at work can be a truly healthy ADDiction. They get all the problem solving  and multitasking their brain needs to be happy, but then they clock out of work at a defined time.

I could write an entire chapter on just this one ADDiction.

"I'm addicted to exercise." *Dave M.*

This ADDiction is another perfect example of a positive and a negative and is more common than one might think. First, the positive: several things happen when you exercise, especially if you get your heart rate into the aerobic zone for at least 30 minutes. In addition to the countless physical benefits, exercise can have psychological benefits. Studies show that exercise can increase the amounts of the neurotransmitters dopamine and serotonin in your brain. These increased levels can help treat disorders such as Parkinson's disease and depression, as well as increase focus and help you feel more energetic overall. Serotonin and dopamine are found in antidepressant medications as well as in amphetamines, the drugs used to "cure" ADHD, but when produced naturally in the body, serotonin and dopamine don't come with all the negative side affects commonly associated with amphetamine use and or abuse.

You may have heard of "the runner's high." Well, I'm here to tell you that it's real, it's all natural, and it's healthy. Dopamine and serotonin generally create a feeling of euphoria, mental focus, and resilience against physical fatigue.

Try some! It can be picked up at your local running store in the form of good shoes, and taken in 30 minute doses daily or as needed for good focus and well-being.

The negative: exercise in excess can detract from other important life activities. My twin brother loves to exercise, and many would call him an addict (he is, after all, ADHD as well.) He chooses the gym and lifting weights; I choose running. He works out sometimes twice a day, and it can be excessive. With running, it's almost impossible for me to work out too much—cramps, dehydration, and even blisters will put an end to my workouts even if I *want* to keep going. Running workouts have a defined finish, forced by physical side effects of going too long. Working out with weights can be difficult to keep in check, though, because once you work one muscle group to fatigue you can just move on to another muscle group. The workout could go for hours. If you're retired and have no family, maybe that's okay. Otherwise, be careful: gym workouts could easily become an unhealthy ADDiction.

Mark and his son, Connor, after a 5K.

Running is my personal healthy ADDiction of choice. If I need a mental break, I listen to a good book or talk radio when I run, so I keep the brain engaged. Or sometimes I'll head out with a problem I need to solve and let my mind pick it apart as I run. Win-win, either way.

"I'm addicted to movies." *Ken P.*

I have to laugh at this one. I am totally addicted to movies. Movies engage the brain on many levels. Mysteries, or "whodunits" are particularly good for the problem-solving ADHD brain. We will drive people nuts sitting next to us because we'll be whispering in their ear who the villain is before the movie is halfway done. One reason this is a healthy ADDiction is because it has **a defined start and finish.**

T. V. CAUTION: Beware the series! *Lost*, 24, etc. can become total distraction ADDictions. I purposely avoided *Lost* until I could take a week off from work just to watch all the episodes. I know I'm a movie ADDict, so I plan accordingly and keep it healthy.

"I'm addicted to sporting events" *Ryan T.*

What defines sports addiction is not how much time you spend watching each week, it's whether or not that time is causing negative behavior in your life. If you're tuning in to watch games in spite of your wife threatening to leave you, your bills going unpaid, and your laundry piled to the ceiling, then you may have an addiction.

-ProfessorsHouse.com

This is just like the movie ADDiction—it's healthy, as long as you keep it in check. Watching a game, using your rapid-fire brain to analyze the players involved, the strategies, the rules, etc., is right up the ADHD alley. I would suggest NOT signing up for the Sports Packages your local cable or satellite provider is offering, though. Healthy Addictions can become unhealthy oh, so fast.

"I'm addicted to praise/accolades." *Jason B*.

Well, if that doesn't drive someone to extreme levels of success, I'm not sure what will. However, it saddens me because this ADDiction usually stems from low self-worth. Those with ADHD are, more often than not, people-pleasers by nature. They're top performers at work, have a healthy competitive spirit, were maybe even the class clown in school, etc., and that's all fine. But when it's compounded by a need to prove value to others it's not a healthy ADDiction. Awesome results, yes. But healthy? NO! I believe, in large part, it's common in those with ADHD because of the "Attention Deficit Hyperactivity Disorder" label we have been burdened with. Until we cast out those I'm-broken-because-an-expert-said-so beliefs, we will never find the healthy side of this ADDiction, which is, incidentally, the most prevalent of the healthy ADDictions, and follows below.

"I'm addicted to success." *Andrea A.*

Oh, what a wonderful and healthy ADDiction. This was one of the most common ADDictions mentioned by the ADDers, and it was completely and entirely unsolicited. Success, however you define it, breeds success. It is its own motivator, and it

> "SUCCESS CAN, AND SHOULD, BE MEASURED BY THE SMALL THINGS THAT YOU DO, LIKE MAKING A GOAL TO WAKE UP ON TIME AND THEN DOING IT, DAY BY DAY."

comes with its own addictive, and yet somehow healthy chemical, adrenaline. It's insatiable, and yet still completely satisfying at the same time. Once you get hooked, there is almost no turning back, and yet success has no negative side effects. Those ADDers who find this ultimate ADDiction thrive in almost every area of their lives. One individual's definition of success needs not be another's, and should never be imposed on anyone else. For me, success at home is my ADDiction. Someone else's ADDiction might be their pursuit of an education, and yet another's in their pursuit of wealth. Many define success by some religious or philanthropic measurement. To each individual, his or her own definition of success must be granted. I only hope we can all find this ever-abundant ADDiction to success and share it with others.

I need to make something very clear concerning success. Success, by no means, needs to be measured by size or grandeur. It can, and should, be measured by the small things that you do, like making a goal to wake up on time and then doing it, day by day. Excellent! For a child, remembering her backpack before leaving for school can be a huge success, and should be celebrated. In recognizing these little triumphs, you're building self-worth brick by brick—yours, your child's, anyone's. And it works because it's recognition for something that was *actually accomplished*. Small successes are perfect opportunities for you to practice being that Equal-Opposite that you or someone else needs, too. For example, a Normal might come down on a child for the one day out of the week that she forgot her backpack. An Equal-Opposite, though, would focus on how *awesome* it is that she remembered it the other four days. Which do you think would be the more effective reminder? The small successes breed larger successes. Recognize that, and celebrate!

I know someone is thinking it, so I'll ask it for you. Can an ADDiction to Success go too far? Yes, but only if you don't sit down and decide for yourself what YOUR definition of success is. Undefined, you'll only treat it like another problem to be solved, and you'll spend *way* too much time trying to figure it out, moving from one thing to another. So define it, define you, and let that ADDictive personality, that problem-solving genius inside you, get to work on it.

I have two more addiction confessions to share with you, but these are from interviews with the ADDicts. I think they're *very* telling. The first one comes from Casey B., who after telling me about his unhealthy ADDictions (drugs—lots of 'em), shared this with me:

"I'm also addicted to photography." *Casey B.*

Casey told me that looking through that lens, trying to capture all of the elements of the shot, is soothing to him. Soothing is right. As an addiction, photography involves more than enough to engage an ADHD brain (three, even four dimensions to keep in mind: aperture, shutter speed, image, emotional intent, etc.) And when we're engaged, we're calm (relatively speaking). Incredibly challenging, very healthy.

Sadly, Casey had lumped all of his addictions together, not realizing how healthy photography really is. To him, an addiction was just an addiction. What he didn't realize was that photography could have been his ONLY addiction. The ADHD brain is all about engagement, and if he would only have poured everything into photography, he wouldn't have needed to self-medicate with drugs. The good news is that if you're still alive it's never too late.

"I'm addicted to failure." *Derek H.*

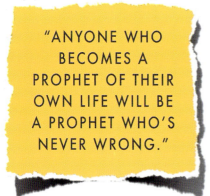

"ANYONE WHO BECOMES A PROPHET OF THEIR OWN LIFE WILL BE A PROPHET WHO'S NEVER WRONG."

Words fail me. Okay, not really—I wouldn't be me if that was true. But honestly, this addiction is tragic because it's so prevalent in today's society. How does a person—a living, breathing miracle—become addicted to failure? I have a theory. Follow along with me: once someone is diagnosed as having Attention Deficit Disorder, they latch on to that label and all it implies. Again, "deficit," "disorder," . . . what more do they need to hear? Once they're convinced that they're damaged, there's not much to aspire to. From there, they'll keep sabotaging any chance they have of success, because who are they to do anything right? They're *broken*. Anyone who becomes a prophet of their own life will be a prophet who's never wrong. After they're diagnosed as disordered, and once they buy in to the idea that they're broken, they will live up (or down) to every prophecy they make about themselves.

There's so much in the world to engage us, good and bad. But I'm hoping at this point you're thinking, "Well, if I'm going to be addicted to anything, I'd rather be addicted to something constructive!" There are lots of healthy addictions out there, but only a few that will fit both the ADHD personality and you. Start looking for and testing your own healthy addictions, and eliminate the unhealthy addictions in your life. And when possible, modify any unhealthy addictions so that they can become healthy—plan out your work day, tone down your workouts, get rid of cable TV, etc. And most importantly, understand and believe that you are NOT broken! Far, far from it.

You've got endless options.
Pick good ones.

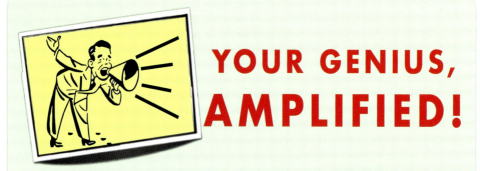

YOUR GENIUS, AMPLIFIED!

The Way to Optimize Healthy Addictions

In case I didn't make it clear in the chapter, the best way to pick up and actually keep a Healthy ADDiction is to make it completely yours. What I mean by that is

find something that YOU enjoy doing!

Not your friend, brother, sister, mother, father, eccentric neighbor-you. Does that sound obvious? Well, yeah, it does. But people have an innate desire to fit in, so they'll often gravitate towards activities that they might not otherwise be inclined to do. That's not a bad thing, either-I am ALL for trying new things. That's how undiscovered talents are found. But what if it's something you just honestly don't like? Well, after you've given it a fair shot (and by that I mean that you've also fulfilled any commitments that you've made to a team, club, etc.), then move on to another healthy option. The danger is that if someone tries something because someone else does it, and it just doesn't click, that they give up altogether. That makes an opening for unhealthy addictions to sneak in, because they tend to be WAY easier. So find *YOUR* Healthy ADDiction, and it will be a lifelong source of fulfillment.

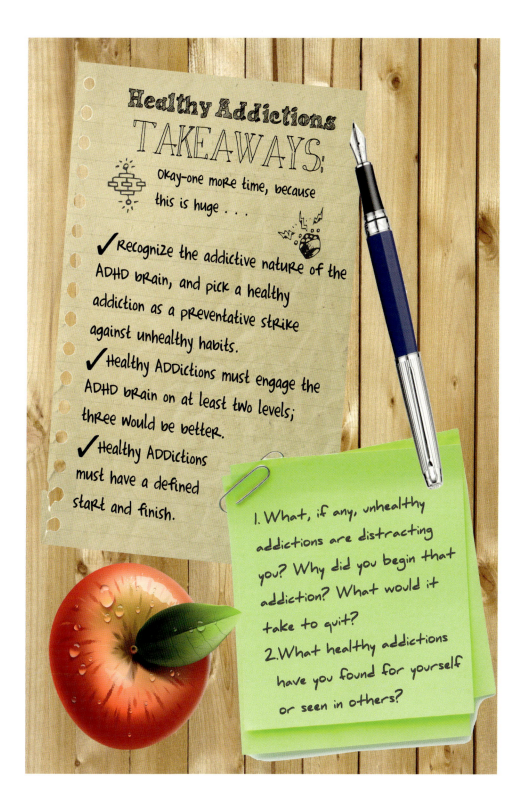

CHAPTER 13

DIFFERENT IS NOT A DISORDER

For centuries, mankind has struggled with things that are different or unusual. We're very often creatures of comfort, and anything out of the ordinary can be intimidating. But it's not just *things* that are different that have made us uncomfortable; we've had a hard time with people who are different, as well. Mighty wars have been started and great nations toppled over something as simple as the color of someone's skin, or in what part of the world they were born. Millions have died over racial conflicts, and that's just the start. Millions more have been slaughtered not because they look different, but simply because they think differently. How dare they have different ideas or beliefs? Certainly, if someone doesn't think as I do, they deserve to die, or at a bare minimum, be torn down, belittled, and ridiculed. There is no room in this world for conflict of thought. Don't believe me? Think of all who have died simply for being part of a different religion. This isn't just a mistake of the past; it continues today.

Conflict as a result of difference in thought, beliefs, ideas, or ideals is a huge challenge, and one might effectively argue that it's a challenge the world might never overcome. But let's take it one step further, and add to the dilemma of difference. What if someone, or even a group of people, actually *think* differently? I'm not talking about ideas or beliefs here—what if they actually process information in their brains in a different way than 93% of the world's population? What if they learn differently? Brainstorm differently? What if they process info in different parts of their brains than everyone else? And what if one could actually see those differences under modern brain-scanning technologies? History teaches us that these "different" individuals would be labeled as inferiors, and treated as such. And sadly, history has repeated itself.

> **DiSTRACTiON:**
> Men and women are different. No, really. But that's not necessarily a bad thing. In fact, it explains a lot . . .
> ✓ Women are more complex than men. This is based on research printed in the Los Angeles Times. The reason? Men have both an X and a Y chromosome, but genetic instructions are only found on the X chromosome. Therefore, women receive twice the amount of genetic instructions as men do, and that makes them more complex than men.
> ✓ Men are faster than women. However, research cited in Nature confirms that the time difference between men's and women's speed in a 100-meter race has been decreasing over time.
> ✓ Women use about 3.5 times more words in a day as men do (7,000 compared to 2,500).
> -psychtronic.com

I'm told I have Attention Deficit Disorder. According to that most reliable of sources, Wikipedia:

*A **deficit** is the amount by which a sum falls short of some reference amount. Cognitive deficit is any characteristic that acts as a barrier to cognitive performance.*

Wow. "Deficit" is a mighty damning label. Then add to it:

*A **disorder** is an abnormal condition negatively affecting the body of an organism.*

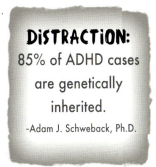

DiSTRACTiON:
85% of ADHD cases are genetically inherited.
-Adam J. Schweback, Ph.D.

Pow! No hope for me; I might as well give up now. Based on those definitions, maybe we shouldn't even ride on the same bus as other kids, but have a bus all to ourselves. We probably shouldn't take advanced classes; we should be in a special class. And forget about getting the same jobs; leave that to the smart people. After all, we are inferior and just need to accept it. To treat us as anything different isn't doing us any favors.

I recently visited one of my closest and dearest friends, Jeremiah Johnson. (Yes, movie buffs, that's his real name. Awesome, right?) Miah was showing me a hen house and pen he had built in his back yard. It was exciting for him and his family to get natural, fresh eggs daily. He was also happy about the idea of teaching his kids responsibility. Caring for the hens, feeding them, cleaning the pen, etc. would all be priceless life lessons learned through this experience. And it worked out that way, until one day when the kids came in screaming and crying. One of the new additions to the flock was being attacked, the hen born with a red dot in its feathers. The other chickens had apparently discovered it, and were pecking at the dot. That chicken was different than they were. Interestingly, when the hen was against the fence and the dot was not visible, they left it alone and it could sit and quietly recover from the previous attack. But once the dot was visible, the pecking resumed. In the end, in order to save the hen's life they colored the dot. It is not an unusual thing for chickens and hens to peck each other to death. It's where the term "pecking order" comes from. They will often attack and kill the ones that are different. So it is with ADHD. We often hide our true colors as a defense mechanism, and simply sit out our lives on the sideline hoping to avoid the pain of being different.

I argue that **different is not a disorder**, and labeling it as such is as ignorant as any form of bigotry. I acknowledge that we are different, and with those differences come unique challenges. I weep for parents who struggle to raise ADHD children without the proper tools and understanding. I'm sympathetic to teachers and educators who are limited to curriculum and teaching environments painstakingly tailored over centuries for best results for the 93%. I understand why they feel they need to do it that way. Caring for and teaching those with ADHD can definitely be a challenge. However, Attention Deficit Hyperactivity Disorder is far more painful for those 7% who have it than it is challenging for parents and teachers. Who's the real victim in this life story—the parent or teacher burdened with an ADHD child, or the child who becomes the victim of ignorance?

The angler fish - it's different, but it eats well.

I want to shift gears and talk for a second about horses, and in particular, the horse's ass. (And since I'm writing the book, I get to.) The two most recognized horses on the planet are the clydesdale and the quarter horse. The clydesdale is a huge, powerful creature that dwarfs all other horses in size and strength, and has been famous for pulling the Budweiser carriage in parades and television ads for decades. The quarter horse is a lean, mean, running machine. Well known for being one of the fastest animals on the planet, it can gallop at nearly 44 mph with a passenger on its back. Both

of these animals have four legs, are covered in fur, come in similar colors, and of course, are both horses. But if anyone took a clydesdale and put it in the starting gate at the Kentucky Derby, others might call him a horse's ass and laugh at him for being the fool that he is. And if you took a quarter horse and hitched it up to a suds wagon, you'd be making the same mistake. Yet this is exactly what we do to those with ADHD. A horse is a horse and people are people? Bull crap! (Edited for young readers.) We are different, and **different is not a disorder!** Train a clydesdale like a clydesdale should be trained, and a quarter horse like a quarter horse.

I celebrate my unique differences and look to nature as my inspiration in that celebration. My brain is as hyperactive as my body. Scratch that, my brain is about ten times more hyperactive than my body ever was, even when I was a "wiggle butt" in elementary school. My brain sprints from place to place, rapidly moving from one curiosity to the next, learning, even devouring information it finds interesting at the time. My sprinting brain, to many (and even to me in my early years), seemed chaotic. However, I've learned it is not chaos at all, just rapid. As random as it may appear, whenever I track its leaping from topic to topic, it always has a connection, and it's always looking for connections, exploring the relationship between completely random things. My greatest inventions came from my ADHD brain and a pile of junk; what seemed like chaos was a prerequisite to creativity. This is a gift that should be magnified, encouraged, even taught and trained to work, or run, if you will, even faster than it does naturally. It should not be taught to slow down, or to pull a cart. It can, but that is not what Mother Nature intended for it.

YOUR GENIUS, AMPLIFIED!

The takeaway message here? Don't be a horse's ass. Einstein once said,

> *"Everybody is a genius, but if you judge a fish by its ability to climb a tree, it will live its whole life believing that it is stupid."*

Add to that the inspiring words of Frank Zappa,

> *"Without deviation from the norm, progress is not possible."*

I embrace who I am, with all my differences, and I embrace any who find themselves on the outside of "normal." I implore you to celebrate the gifts of ADHD with me; accept them, love them, learn to magnify and strengthen them. For when the time comes, and the gate opens, you will have put yourself on the right track, ready to run with others like us; at full speed.

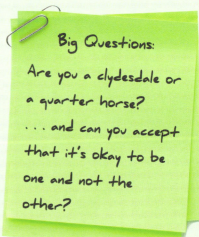

Big Questions:

Are you a clydesdale or a quarter horse?

... and can you accept that it's okay to be one and not the other?

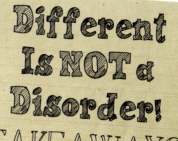

Different Is NOT a Disorder!

TAKEAWAYS:

✓ We all have different abilities.

✓ Our differences need to be embraced and celebrated, magnified and strengthened.

✓ Not another brick in the wall—thank goodness!

Everybody is a genius. But if you judge a fish by its ability to climb a tree, it will live its whole life believing that it is stupid.

Albert Einstein.

"My greatest inventions came from my ADHD brain and a pile of junk. What seemed like chaos was a prerequisite to creativity. This is a gift that should be magnified and encouraged."

-Mark Patey

CHAPTER 14

PUSHING LIMITS

> "Oh #*@%! - not the turbo clamps again!"

DISTRACTION: The Pateys' race planes fly at up to 400 m.p.h. (!)

After slaving over the race planes for weeks they are finally ready. Boost controllers modified, mixture tweaked, propeller RMPs adjusted, oil changed and filters cleaned. Mike and I are looking forward to the air race in Texas the next morning, and it would be the first race we would ever do together in two different planes. The excitement was further amplified due to our recent success—setting a new Transcontinental World Speed Record—in these very aircraft. Our hopes were high that our race season opener would begin with the Patey twins taking first and second place. A lofty goal considering the tough competition this year, but boys can dream; besides, if you're going to aim, aim high and push it hard. Also, having ADHD gives you an incredible imagination, making it very easy for the two of us to imagine all kinds of fun things, like the conversations people would have about us if we won like that. The respect, new friends, chatter on the internet forums. . . . (Wow, I really crave accolades.) I even imagined there would be a mean and arrogant competitor who would say hateful things about us and tell us we didn't belong there. That way we could win in true Disney-movie form and make the bad guy look stupid, then maybe we would become life-long friends and he would turn out to be not such a bad guy after all. :) (I don't know what it is about needing a naysayer to win over. Seems like there needs to be a chase to push us to our full potential.)

The Patey Bros. pushing limits in their self-built Lancairs.

So, the planes are ready, we're at the fuel pump topping the tanks for the 2.5 hour flight from our home airport in Spanish Fork, UT to Texoma, TX. Oh, and I have to say there is nothing like the smell of aviation gasoline before a flight. Mmmm . . . smells like fun! Turning money into fuel into noise—it's just magical. Our conversation continues to be about the fun of What if we won? What if we tied for first? WHAT IF we beat the North American P-51 Mustang that's rumored to show up!?! I have to point out: ADHD minds don't spend much time on the negative when we are trying to accomplish something fun, new, exciting, or "shiny." More often than not, we are blind optimists. It's a blessing and a curse. The only negative thing we talked about was pushing the planes up to max race power settings before we got into the mountains. If a plane is going to fail, statistically it's going to happen when at max power on take off, or racing on the course. We both have had engine failures before, and had no desire to make an "engine-out" landing during the race, or even worse, when crossing the unforgiving Rocky Mountains (there just aren't many survivable places there to put down a plane that lands at nearly 100 m.p.h.). We both agreed we would do a max power test while still in gliding distance and altitude from the airport before crossing the Rockies, and with that we climbed into the planes and pushed the Make Noise Buttons, AKA the Big Smiles Buttons, and the engines roared to life.

Ranch Prat, a business partner of mine, was along for the ride and and some weekend fun. Ranch and I have a great relationship, and after building several companies together we can say it like it is with each other without the usual worries of offending or overstepping bounds. This would prove to be one of those times.

After making the standard radio calls to alert other aircraft in the area of our intentions, we took the runway for departure. Once lined up with the centerline, I pushed the go lever forward and felt the 580-cubic inch, twin-turbo-charged fire breather roar to life as we sank back in our seats. Everything was perfect. Fuel flows were in line with power settings, oil temp and pressure were both good, boost pressure at a constant 38" manifold pressure. Reaching a nice 100 mph-indicated airspeed, I gently pulled back on the stick, raising the nose to a climb attitude. *No Regrets* (my plane) leaped into the air and started climbing like a homesick angel. I've always lived a high-risk lifestyle, and flying *No Regrets* continually reminds me to live my life without regrets, because any day could be your last.

I circled the airport once to gain a few thousand feet, then pushed the power up to its race setting of 42" manifold pressure. This is the engine manufacturer's maximum allowable power setting, and is about 120% of max continuous cruise power. This power setting is only to be used for takeoff, if needed, or to clear obstacles in the climb, like trees or mountains. For racers and competitive types, this is also where we might set the engine power for racing. Sometimes to win, we may even go beyond this power setting; some will even push to over 200% maximum allowable power.

Continuing my steep climb at 120% power, I pointed the nose toward Spanish Fork Canyon. Within two minutes of takeoff, we were climbing through 10,000 feet MSL (above median see level) and well into the mouth of the canyon. It was at this point that we heard a screaming noise from the engine. The airplane yawed unexpectedly as the power dropped off dramatically. Ranch and I looked at each other with eyes as big as dinner plates. 'Oh #*@%!—not the turbo clamps again!" (This had happened to me before.)

I knew that a turbo clamp failure would cause this kind of power loss, but the screaming noise was new, and it wasn't from Ranch or me. It was my red mistress telling me she was in trouble. Pushing the controls hard to the left, I began an immediate hard turn back toward the airport for an emergency landing. Halfway through the turn I noticed my wingtip pointing at a familiar field in the canyon below. *NO WAY . . . is that where I pulled the dead body out of the burnt airplane a couple years ago?* I couldn't believe what I was seeing, remembering, and currently experiencing.

"We okay? Are we going to make it back to the airport? Or is this really bad?"

It was surreal. What are the odds that my wingtip would point at the very spot I bagged a charcoaled body after a plane crash only a few years earlier? The memories came flooding back, but there was not time to focus on them. Rolling out of the turn, I refocused on my engine monitoring equipment and the situation at hand. Other than a loss of power everything looked okay— the engine was still running, just not very well. I called out over the local airport advisory frequency, "Spanish Fork Area Traffic, Lancair N913MP is on a five mile final straight-in for landing runway thirty."

Another aircraft replied, "N913MP, did you know that you're trailing smoke?!" I twisted like a Twizzler and pressed my face against the window to try to see behind us. Yup . . . we were trailing smoke like nothing I had ever seen.

I replied over the radio, "We've had a failure of some kind and are coming in for an emergency landing." Ranch, never afraid to ask the tough questions, piped up.

"We okay? Are we going to make it back to the airport? Or is this really bad?"

I could hear the stress in his voice, but had to admit he was surprisingly calm, all things considered.

"The engine is still running, and we still have fuel and oil pressure. We should be fine." No sooner were the words out of my mouth than the low oil pressure warning lights came on, and I watched the pressure drop from 60 PSI to 30, 20, 10. The plane holds 12 quarts of oil, and if whatever just broke let 12 quarts pump into the engine cowling in less than two minutes, I'd be in serious risk of a fire. Moreover, with the engine exhaust still hot when landing, there would be no question we would burst into flames, if we weren't already on fire.

There was only one option at this point. I pulled the fuel mixture all the way back to starve the engine of fuel, thus shutting off the engine and giving the exhaust and turbos a chance to cool down before landing. I then turned the fuel pump switch to off, to keep from pumping fuel from my wings into the engine compartment. My racer just became the worlds heaviest glider with wings full to the rim with gas, both seats occupied, and travel packs in the back. Taking another look behind us, I could see that the plane was still trailing smoke. And wouldn't you know it, my left wing was talking to me again. It was pointing again, but now at my neighborhood. It was quite literally pointing at my front door. My wife's Escalade was clearly visible, and she was standing in the driveway as I streaked across the sky in eerie silence, trailing smoke.

Unbeknownst to me, my kids were at the school playground watching me go by, their friends asking why my plane was burning.

Once I was certain I was in gliding distance of the airport, I put my gear in

the down position and shut off all electrical to the aircraft to further protect against fire risk. My landing was one of my better landings, I must say. It helps when you're hyper-focused. We coasted to the end of the runway and onto the taxiway. As we rolled to a stop, I looked back again at the smoke trail. You could see that it completely concealed the view of the runway up until the last one-third of our rollout. Even with the engine off for the last two minutes of flight, it didn't cool down enough to stop smoking until the very last few hundred feet of the ordeal. Climbing out of the plane, I could see the puddle of oil quickly building under the plane. No fire. I shudder to think what might have happened if the engine was still hot when we came to a stop.

Scary? Absolutely. Did the experience end my love affair with flying? Not even close. Here's the point: you will never find someone at the finish line in first place who only gave it half effort. You will never find someone who has earned their success by coasting in life. You will never find a winner who played it safe. You will never find a happy man who won that happiness easily. You have to push the limits. Remember, success leaves clues, and this is one of them. But pushing the limits is risky, even deadly at times. Know your limits, all of them—physical, emotional, mental. In my airplane, my turbo failed *completely*, allowing the oil to be pumped out the open hole where a turbo shaft once was. It was fatigued to the point of failure. The turbo, the very thing that makes over 100% of an engine's displacement power possible, is what failed.

The ADHD mind and personality is exactly the same. It's a turbocharged engine. It is capable of well over 100% power; it can EASILY produce 120%, even 200% of what a normally-aspirated engine can produce, or in other words, what the Normals can produce. However, it can over-boost, overheat, and overload the system. A turbo typically spins at around 100,000 rotations per minute (rpm). Think of this as 100% power. However, the turbo will spin at over 200,000 rpm if you let it, raging past safe limits in only seconds. Spool it up, and it will provide short bursts of power that will blow away the competition. But know when to back it off, slow it up, cool it down. You have to relax from time to time. Take a break, watch a movie, sleep in, whatever works. (Healthy ADDictions!)

I've surrounded myself with Equal-Opposites in every aspect of my life. They know when to hold me back from going full power. It's not that they want to limit me; heck, they want me at a full 200%! They just put safety systems in place to keep me from overheating my turbo.

Mark's newest engine: 780 cubic inch supercharged

At full power, we ADDers are the world's greatest problem solvers: the fastest thinkers, the inventors, the creators, and almost always the first to look at any situation or problem from an entirely new perspective. But chances are, once we catch our own new vision, we might continue, full speed ahead, without a detailed, thought-out, action-itemed game plan. Insert your Equal-Opposite here.

On almost all airplanes, maximum continuous power allowed by the manufacturer is 65%-75% power. I treat myself the same way. This doesn't mean you should be lazy or a slacker. We aren't lazy or slackers by nature, we're sprinters! We just don't know when to slow it down once we get into high boost. It feels so good to get in gear and go fast. In fact, when we start a project, and our internal ADHD turbo spools up, we will go all night long to finish when everyone else has long since shut down and given up for the day. Our blessing and curse is we feed so well on our own success, our progress, that once we are revved up we have an incredible, almost insatiable desire to finish. And that's great! Finish it, but you'd better unplug and rest afterwards.

> *"Boundaries are to protect life, not to limit pleasures."*
> *-Edwin Louis Cole*

Know what your personal limits are. What can your body/engine handle? What can you mentally handle? Moreover, what can your spouse, employer, or business partners handle? Here is the problem: if these people haven't become your Equal-Opposites and understand that valuable role, when you finish your sprint you will feel obligated to jog at the pace the rest of the world is running.

Maybe you were up all night because you got "turboed," and now need to go to work again with everyone else at seven a.m. You can't! After an ADHD sprint—that flash of genius, that productive powerhouse session—you can't go to work with everyone else who is getting up fresh to run an eight-hour marathon. You will collapse. You will frustrate those you seek so much to please. There are sprinters, and there are distance runners. Rarely do you see both. You have just sprinted all night, but if your peers don't understand this, if you don't have an Equal-Opposite that understands how productive you are when you get yourself in high gear, you will find yourself a slave to a time clock that ADDers just don't run well with.

Does this mean you can just sleep in and skip work or school because you were up all night? No, of course not. You need to find out how to live within the world and boundaries you set, and make adjustments knowing what you know about your ADHD self. If you have good Equal-Opposites, this will be very easy to do. If not, you may need to call your boss and let him know what you're up to, that you may not finish until late, and you'll be coming in late in the morning. You may just need to go to bed and miss out on that ADHD sprint. Sad, I know, but we live in this world with others who don't work like we do, and we'd prefer not to lose our jobs, fail our classes, or let down our loved ones.

A good Equal-Opposite will let you rev up when they see you getting into gear, and will even celebrate it because they know how much is going to get done in a very short time. You may not be working on what they wanted you to work on right then, but if you're working on something productive they will let you finish. They know shutting you down is like bringing a big flywheel from full speed to a stop. Once it's stopped, getting it back up to speed again can be very difficult.

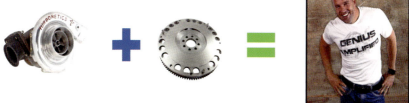

**IF A TURBO MARRIED A FLYWHEEL,
THE CHILD WOULD BE AN ADHD BRAIN.**

Not long ago, my wife asked me to mow the lawn. A simple thirty-minute task, but not much fun. I went to pull the mower out of the garage, and noticed all the gas cans for the ATVs were on the floor and in the way. I picked them up and went out to the enclosed trailer to put them in their place. There I noticed the bikes were still dirty from our last family trip. So I pulled them out to wash them. Once I had the power washer out and running, I thought this would also be a good time to power-wash the garage floor. . . . Long story, short: by three a.m. the garage and trailer were *completely* reorganized, new shelves were installed, labels put on boxes, the hole in the sheetrock fixed and painted, a new radio was installed on the wall for entertainment, the ATVs fueled, tied down, and ready for the next trip, bike hooks installed on the ceiling, tools organized, and for the first time in months, family cars could once again be parked in the garage. The lawn did *not* get mowed—Suzy did it the next morning while I was sleeping in. And she loves that she doesn't park her new car outside anymore.

I was not trying to get out of work, or shrug responsibilities, although a Normal might have seen it that way and become frustrated within minutes of not hearing the mower start up. An Equal-Opposite will understand that the ADHD flywheel is speeding up, and the turbo effect is kicking in to 200% of normal power. They'd let it RUN. In fact, they might even encourage the shift in direction knowing how productive we can be when fully engaged.

A word on motivation:

Those struggling with ADHD may find this chapter foreign. You might even think, *I never get revved-up and motivated like that. I want the ADHD turbo hyper-focused part of me to wake up and get going!*

I understand, and I'm that way too, at times. I find myself saying to friends or family, **"I'm having a hard time getting my motivator started today."** This is usually brought on by a mild depression, lack of sleep, or lack of good nutrition. This is also common for those who find themselves believing the message that ADHD is a disorder. My suggestion? Get some rest, get a good meal in you, read this book again, and find a good E.O. And if all that doesn't help, seek out someone who can work with you on dealing with and overcoming depression. It's real, and nothing to be ashamed of. Preferably, find someone who accepts that ADHD has both challenges and gifts, otherwise they might inadvertently make things worse by further adding to the destructive beliefs in the "incurable ADHD disease."

Pushing Limits
TAKEAWAYS:

1. Work within the boundaries you're currently living in.
2. Ask the Normals in your life to read this book - you just might find them more understanding and willing to allow the ADHD sprints from time to time.
3. Take calculated risks. A good Equal-Opposite is a great help here.
4. Avoid shutting down, if possible, when you're up to full speed on something. We are better off finishing than finding ourselves never getting back to it.
5. Caution: Avoid the temptation to use your "sprinting" nature as an excuse for not working a full and productive day.

CHAPTER 15

NO REGRETS

It's been three months since I last worked on this book. It's been on my mind constantly, and there has been a great deal of internal guilt I've had to deal with whenever anyone asks me if it's finished. It's long overdue, and others are counting on me, so where have I been? Was the three-month break another symptom of my ADHD? I'm laughing inside as I write this... again, I'm writing a book on ADHD, but I got distracted. I'd

Because a regular bridge would be boring.

like to write a book about paranoia but I'm afraid someone will steal my work before I get it published. I'm also going to get a book out on procrastination; I'll get it started tomorrow. I'm sure I could get all books done, plus the book on multiple-personalities if I took a time-management class. But I just can't fit that into my schedule, or into my schedule. Sorry—back to business.

Three months ago, I lost my dearest friend and brother-in-law in a plane crash. My sister's husband, Rob, passed away doing what he loved most. It's been a lot for everyone to deal with. My sister is left with their five young children to raise, and all of us are left wondering why. Should he have been in the air that day? Is there anything that could have been done differently that would have saved them? The details of his death are not important, though. The details of his life, and some conversations I had with him before his passing, are. Rob's mom always said that Rob was born early, hit the ground running, and has never stopped. From experience, I can confirm this is an accurate description of his high-energy, enthusiastic life. He never let a day go by without getting something done, and often for someone else. He was truly unstoppable. I can't help but wonder if he knew somehow that his time on earth would be short, and so he lived every day as if it were his last.

This morning, we opened the hangar door and took Rob's plane out for a short flight. (No, he did not die in his plane—Rob was the passenger in another plane.) Today, December 12, 2012, seemed fitting for a memorial flight in a strange way, because half the world seemed convinced that the Mayans had it right and the world was going to end. But, since the world

Rob Lamb, "Wolverine" flight instructor.

was still turning, we figured that maybe we could renew our goals, reflect on the past, and hold close that which matters most. So we pulled Rob's plane out without him, and took off seeking to find him. And find him we did, in these clear winter skies and in our hearts, as we crossed the Rocky Mountains and shared our closest memories of him.

Only a few short months ago, I was in my hangar working on my plane—my race plane, to be specific. Rob walked in as he always did, with a huge smile and a "Hey Polo, what can I help you with?" (Polo is a nickname Rob gave me twenty-plus years ago.) Rob never came over asking for help, but rather always looking to serve. I told him I needed a name for my plane. Every air race I entered, someone would ask what I called her, and I just hadn't ever come up with anything fitting. Rob laughed, and asked, "How could you have a plane like this and not have her named yet?" I explained that I'd had lots of ideas, and even requested input from Facebook friends when I posted about it once, but nothing seemed fitting. I went over a few with him, and he liked them, but he agreed that they just weren't quite right for a plane I had built myself and put so much blood, sweat, and tears into. After some time, the conversation drifted from fun name ideas to conversations about the dangers of racing aircraft. Finally, he asked straight out, "Polo, do you ever worry about dying when you're out there, pushing the plane to its limits?"

Any excuse for Rob to get airborne . . .

I replied quickly and honestly. "Rob, if there is a God in heaven and it's my time to go, if he loves me, he will take me in my airplane. To die doing what I love, with no pain, and with no regrets." Rob laughed out loud and agreed, adding, "Sounds good to me, as long as you really have lived your life without regrets." His smile grew even more. "There's the name for your plane: NO REGRETS!" It was perfect, and still is—just like my brother-in-law. Thank you, Rob, for your life, your example, and your love. The world is a better place for having had you in it.

I tell Rob's story to explain a little about my absence from writing, but also because it inspires what I'm writing about today: regret, and its close association to the Entitlement Disorder. Regret, born from excuse, raised by laziness and indifference, is a byproduct of the Entitlement Disorder. As you may recall, the Entitlement Disorder is a disease that feeds upon itself, forever impeding those afflicted with it. It's not classified as an actual disorder (though it should be), but rather it's a name I was forced to come up with to help me better describe what I increasingly see in people who work for me, or are interviewing for work. I fear it's a plague of near biblical proportions, and seems to have no cure. It spreads like a mutating virus; simply by socializing with others inflicted with it, you run the risk of catching the disease yourself.

The Entitlement Disorder has reached full maturity when someone takes on the victim role for not receiving something they never earned in the first place. Anyone with the Entitlement Disorder will never see themselves as lazy. They use the actions of others, rather than their own inaction, as an excuse for their life's circumstances, thus trapping them in a cycle of dependency. They remain forever stagnant, waiting for someone else to fix their problems. The outcome is predictable: anger, depression, and a lashing out at those "responsible."

> I would rather be ashes than dust!
> I would rather that my spark should burn out in a brilliant blaze than it should be stifled by dry-rot.
> I would rather be a superb meteor, every atom of me in magnificent glow, than a sleepy and permanent planet.
> The function of man is to live, not to exist.
> I shall not waste my days trying to prolong them.
> I shall use my time.
> -Jack London

Nobody is immune to this disease. It's easily caught, and is particularly contagious for those of us with ADHD. We are more susceptible to this viral thinking because we've already been given an excuse for our behavior, or more appropriately, our misbehavior. We are almost expected to act out. Parents will say, "Yeah, well, he's ADHD," as if it's not only an excuse for our behavior but an excuse for their own lack of parenting. Teachers can be just as guilty as parents for the incubation of this disease by buying in to the stereotype, and allowing students to handicap themselves. Give anyone, ADHD or not, an excuse for misbehavior and the misbehavior will not only continue, **it will increase**. On top of being handed an excuse ("But I'm ADHD"), once the label's attached, nobody expects greatness. I've even heard a parent say, "Forget good grades—I'd be happy if he just passed the class." Behind almost every successful person you will find someone that believed in them, and often, believed in them even more than they believed in themselves.

Imagine, if you would, a football player sitting on the bench at a junior high school game. The game is going well and the home team is well ahead. The parent of the bench-sitter taps the coach on the shoulder, winks at his son, and says to the coach, "Hey, we got a great lead here! How about putting my boy in for some playing time?" The coach looks over at the boy and says, "Put him in the game?!? I'm thrilled if he can sit there without falling off his seat." The parent looks at his boy, and says "You know son, he's probably right. Try not to embarrass any of us. But on the bright side, at least you got to wear the uniform!" So it is in many cases with ADHD. "Don't expect anything from us, and we will do our best not to embarrass you. We will play the game of life, in our minds, from the sideline." That's nuts! Don't expect less, expect more! We are crazy-creative, instinctive, energetic, and have a lot to offer. But we need our Equal-Opposites to see us as equals, and to expect, even demand, more from us than we ourselves thought possible. Does that mean we have to be the star quarterback? Nope. We just need to be the best we can be, with no excuses for who we are. Sure, it's tough to be "diagnosed" as being "disordered," but we don't have to let it feed into an Entitlement Disorder.

Eleanor Roosevelt nailed it with this one:

"No one can make you feel inferior without your consent."

Don't let anyone tell you you've got a free pass to misbehave. We don't need a crutch, we need wings. The good news is, we've already got them. We are all angels in embryo.

Live a life with no regrets—tomorrow may be your last.

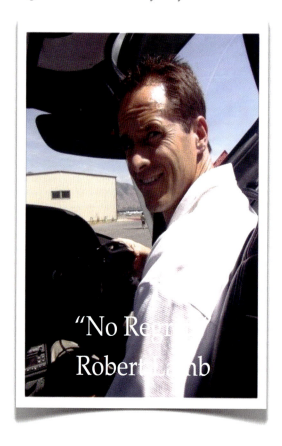

CHAPTER 16

DARK NIGHTS AND A NEW HORIZON

I know nothing absolute. I understand that all my beliefs are little more than the sum of what I've experienced in life, as seen through the filters created by my education. My education came through my family at home, my teachers in school, the faith I was raised in, and the country and culture in which I was born, and all the aforementioned can be, and most certainly are, flawed. An understanding that our life, and everything in it, is seen through the imperfect beliefs we have adopted over time from an imperfect world and imperfect people makes it impossible for any sane human to see anything they "know" to be true as anything more than imperfect. Everything must be suspect. Consequently, only by a willingness to be humble, a willingness to be wrong, and a deep internal commitment to search for truth and align with it can anyone hope to increase and improve. Certainly, an individual who believes himself to be the smartest one in a room full of people is the biggest fool of them all, for he has damned his own progression the moment he arrogantly convinced himself of his own superior insight and knowledge.

We are made up of our beliefs—all our beliefs, both true and false. Every action or inaction is the direct result of what we believe about the subject and/or ourselves. If you want to make a change in your life you must adjust what you believe. That adjustment takes courage, it takes a willingness to be wrong, a willingness to change what you previously "knew" to be true. There is no room for pride, only humility, in the classroom of life if you want to graduate with honors.

In this book, I have attempted to shift your beliefs about ADHD in a direction I've found to be more accurate and healthy than what I was taught growing up. It is my hope that in some way you have shifted your beliefs sufficiently to impact your behavior in a positive way. It is my firm conviction that what I have discovered about myself and ADHD is true; it has certainly brought me success and happiness, not just *where* I am in life, but most importantly, with *who* I am and who I hope to become in the future (a slightly less-flawed version of me).

I want to end this book where I started, with a personal story. Yes, I'm big on those. But again, my experiences are what have shaped me. And this particular experience shaped me profoundly.

I received a phone call from the Utah County Sheriff's Office Search and Rescue about fifteen minutes before sundown at the end of a cool, breezy day. A boat had gone down in Utah Lake after violent winds picked up and unexpectedly capsized the craft. Six souls were on board. One made it to shore safely after over two hours of swimming, five were still missing. I jumped into my helicopter to join the search. There was just enough daylight to get over the lake and find the debris pattern: floating boat cushions, some plastic bottles, life jackets and trash all showed the obvious point where the boat went down and where the wind was pushing the flotsam. After calling in a GPS location and magnetic heading toward shore, I was forced to land due to lack of visibility.

Rescue 1, ready to roll.

Once on the ground I launched into the search with dozens of other boats and watercraft in hopes of finding more survivors. As the night wore on, a second victim was found, alive. He was hypothermic and in really bad shape, but alive. Another hour passed and another was found, nearly dead, floating on his back with a seat cushion under him to keep him up as he had no life jacket. When warmed up and finally speaking coherently, he mentioned he didn't know if the other three got their life vests on or not. The boat had come up one large wave, dove into the next, and was gone, instantly. Anyone with a life vest would have it only if they found it floating up from the sunken vessel.

Hopes for the last three faded fast. The water temperature was too low to be survivable for any longer than the time that had already passed. Just then, all lights on the boat I was on went out. The overcast night was as black as a dark cave, with the only light coming from the city on the distant shore and the swarm of rescue boats spread all over the search area. We tried everything to get the lights back, but nothing worked. All the breakers were good, switches seemed to be fine, and we had power. Just no lights, for no apparent reason, on a brand new boat. We felt helpless and frustrated. Just then I remembered some night vision goggles a friend had left in my hangar to use if I ever needed them on a rescue. We made the decision to head back to shore and retrieve the goggles so we could continue with the search.

The trip back to shore was slower than molasses on a cold day. Without lights, we were forced to cruise all the way in at a painstakingly slow, wakeless speed as to not inadvertently kill one of the three remaining victims. Just then, a call came over the radios: a forth victim had just been pulled out of the water, alive, but with a core body temperature below the "survivable" limits. Comments were made on our boat that this was going to turn from a search-and-rescue effort into a recovery effort.

With two still remaining, and in an attempt to be productive, I called and woke up my wife Suzy, and asked her if she could quickly get the night vision goggles and bring them down to the lake. She informed me that a close friend of mine, Brian, had borrowed them to go hunting in Alaska. I was sick, even a little angry, inside. What if someone died tonight who we could have saved? I told Suzy to call Brian and ask if he had, in fact, taken the goggles with him.

Suzy replied with a little frustration. "I was there when he picked up the goggles; he is in Alaska, and it's three a.m. I'm not waking him up in the middle of the night to find out what I already know. Besides, he said he would be out of cell phone coverage for the next three days."

This news should have been devastating, but it somehow wasn't. I simply asked again, and used an unarguable argument.

"Suzy, this is life and death! Please, call Brian."

She agreed to make an effort. Only a few minutes later she called me back, now wide awake and filled with adrenalin.

"Brian answered the phone! He tried to tell me he didn't have much of a signal and the call would drop but asked what I needed. When I told him you needed the goggles, he said he had packed the goggles, but as he was walking out the front door to leave his house he had a bad feeling."

Apparently, the thought entered Brian's mind, *What if Mark ends up needing these?* Despite over two years of the goggles never being needed on a rescue, he pulled them out of his baggage and told Suzy he had placed them at his front door.

What if the last victims somehow swam the wrong way, and had to watch the world searching for them in the wrong place?

Suzy was on her way to his house as we spoke. We met at the Provo boat harbor at exactly the same time. We pulled in, she handed over the goggles and we backed out in about ten seconds. Now equipped with vision, we roared back out on our search at full speed. The boat was still without lights, and everyone on board was blind, but I could see everything clearly through those green-colored lenses. Somehow the goggles filter out the darkness and present only the visible light, and then magnify that light into something we can interpret.

The driver of the boat was nervous, and understandably so. He was forced to put his trust in a guy on the front of his boat yelling back, "Full speed ahead, the way is clear!" Even though he himself could see nothing but blackness, he pushed ahead at full throttle. As we neared the search area, I could clearly see all the other search vessels combing the site. They looked like busy ants working a scrap of bread. As I panned left, I saw only dark waves and an enormous empty lake, and I could feel the emptiness creep into my soul. Panning back again straight ahead toward the lights of the city, I could see all the boats between us and the shore so clearly. At that moment, a thought entered my mind and my heart sank:

What if the last victims somehow swam the wrong way, and had to watch the world searching for them in the wrong place?

I panned back again toward the middle of the lake. The blackness nearly brought tears to my eyes as I thought of how hopeless and helpless I would feel if I were out there.

I told the boat driver, "Let's search outside of the search area. We can cover so much more ground now with night vision, and nobody's checked toward the middle of the lake." Several people on the boat made comments along the lines of "What's the point? Nobody would swim away from shore." But after some encouragement, the group was convinced we could give it five minutes before joining everyone else.

Five minutes went by with nothing in sight, and I felt like a fool for pointing us so far away from where the survivors were found. Just as I was about to ask to turn the boat around, I spotted what looked like a small ball bobbing in and out of the water. With some coaching to the driver, we were able to come up alongside the object. It was one of the victims, his head back in the water with only his face showing. It was immediately obvious he was dead. His mouth was slacked open, face and ears were swollen and waterlogged to the point that he didn't look human, and his skin was that distinctive pasty gray that only comes from a human body with no heartbeat.

One of the other rescuers held a bright flashlight on the victim so we wouldn't lose him as we positioned the boat to retrieve the body. Just as we got close enough to reach out for him his eyes opened. It scared the crap out of me! He didn't look at anyone or anything, his eyes never moved, he didn't even blink. But something was still going on in that brain. I reached over the boat to grab him, but just then a wave hit. His head went facedown into the water, and there was no effort on his part to lift his head out. In a panic, I reached out and barely got a hold of the shoulder of his life jacket. I dragged him toward the boat where the other rescuers could get a good grip. In one swift motion he was onto the boat, lake water spewing from his lungs.

At full speed toward the shore we called in to base.

"One soul on board, critical condition, faint pulse, faint breathing, unconscious." The team wrapped he and I tightly into some insulation blankets to bring his core body temperature up, in hopes of increasing his breathing and pulse. I remember thinking to myself, "How can this guy still be alive? Will he live though the night? If he lives, will he be a vegetable? Did we get to him in time?"

Days passed, and we were still searching for the last victim. We knew there was no chance he was alive; it was a recovery effort for the family. I was in the chopper looking for the body, which should have been floating back up to the surface by then. However, about halfway though my grid search I was called back to base. They said someone was there to see me and I should come right back. Upon landing I could see from a distance a young man, standing on his own two feet, surrounded by his family and relatives, looking vastly different than he had last time I had seen him. It was the fifth survivor. I couldn't believe he was out of the hospital, as the last word I had heard was that he was touch-and-go. His kidneys had been on the verge of failure from processing all the dead body tissue created by lack of blood flow to his extremities.

As I approached I was greeted first by some of his family, thanking us for saving his life. He said nothing as his family members took turns explaining how he had nearly started a fight to get released from the hospital so he could come down to the lake. He wanted to say thanks, and to be there when his brother's body was recovered. I was torn between heartbreak for his loss, and celebration for what I was told would eventually be a full recovery.

He still hadn't said anything himself, so I broke his silence with simple small talk.

"Do you remember us pulling you out of the lake?"

He shook his head in the negative.

I continued to probe. "Do you remember the boat ride, or the ambulance?"

Again, he shook his head.

I asked one final question. "What's the last thing you remember from that night?"

No one could have prepared me for his answer.

He teared up as he thought for a moment, then replied,

"The buckles."

"The buckles?" I asked, looking at his family for clarification that what I heard what right.

The women were suddenly crying outright, and even the roughest-looking members in the group looked like they were willing their tears back. I was confused.

"What do you mean, 'The buckles?' I don't understand."

He explained that while floating in the water, the pain was so great as his body shut down, the agony was so unbearable, and the darkness around him so complete, that he couldn't take it anymore. So he tried to undo his life jacket buckles to free himself from the suffering, the loneliness he felt. But his fingers wouldn't work. The last bit of his conscious awareness was a struggle, even a fight, to undo his buckles and find release.

The story above is true, but not just the story of a boat sinking on a lake in Utah. This story is true for millions struggling with ADHD. There are kids and adults who feel like the world has left them alone in the dark. Broken and afraid, unable to help themselves, they are giving up hope. It's dark, lonely, and sometimes seems like an impossible battle hardly worth fighting. The reality is this: when the pain is great enough, and you see the rest of the world like city lights in the distance, and everyone that is searching to help you is searching in the wrong place, eventually it is easier to give up. I never asked this young man how he ended up swimming so far in the wrong direction, but it hardly matters. Nor does it matter how the ADHD world has ended up off course. What matters is that we do whatever it takes to get it back on course.

To all who read this book: I implore you—on bended knee, I beg—join in this search-and-rescue effort. We need you. There are more than enough people telling us about the problems we have. But we already know; we live with them. We need people fighting to promote the positives, fighting for the lives of those lost and struggling alone in the dark.

In many ways, we are all that airplane pilot in the opening chapter of this book. For whatever reason, at times we've all thought we were okay and on the right course, until conditions suddenly got rough. When we find we're losing altitude, are we humble enough to call out and ask for help? Who is your air traffic controller? Are we tuned in to the right frequency to get a hold of Him? Will we change course when told by that quiet, but confident, voice over the headset? Because when the time comes, we will have to fly this plane, or drive this boat, to the end of our journey. Once there, we will all ask ourselves:

How many souls on board?

Only in following your instincts and the intuitive responses from within can you best judge which of life's lessons are worth adopting. There are so many conflicting ideas, ideals, and ideologies. Don't let anyone tell you you're not complete. Don't allow any diagnosis to make you feel like you're broken. Don't let any "expert" convince you that you're disordered. Don't let anyone persuade you to make destructive choices. In other words, you are your own pilot; do not let anyone else fly your plane. And just as there are those who would drag you down, understand that the resources and information, the knowledge, and the partners you need to truly take charge and take flight are out there and readily available. It's up to you.

Choose your course wisely.

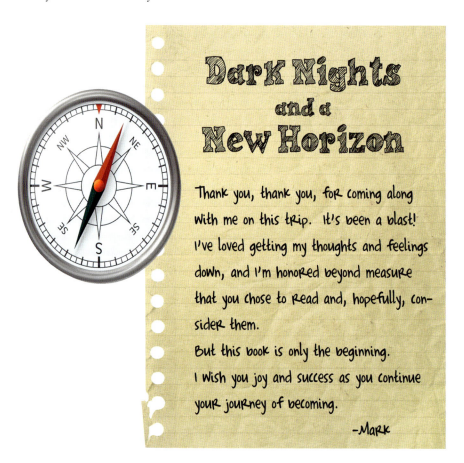

Dark Nights and a New Horizon

Thank you, thank you, for coming along with me on this trip. It's been a blast! I've loved getting my thoughts and feelings down, and I'm honored beyond measure that you chose to read and, hopefully, consider them.

But this book is only the beginning.

I wish you joy and success as you continue your journey of becoming.

—Mark

What impacted you the most? Let us know!

theadhdgift@gmail.com